Building Wealth, Financial Freedom and Debt-Free Living for Families

The Ultimate Guide for Families to Successfully Manage Money and Finances, Stay Out of Debt and Build Generational Wealth

Lincoln Allen

© Copyright 2021 - All rights reserved.

The content contained within this book may not be reproduced, duplicated or transmitted without direct written permission from the author or the publisher.

Under no circumstances will any blame or legal responsibility be held against the publisher, or author, for any damages, reparation, or monetary loss due to the information contained within this book, either directly or indirectly.

Legal Notice:

This book is copyright protected. It is only for personal use. You cannot amend, distribute, sell, use, quote or paraphrase any part, or the content within this book, without the consent of the author or publisher.

Disclaimer Notice:

Please note the information contained within this document is for educational and entertainment purposes only. All effort has been executed to present accurate, up to date, reliable, complete information. No warranties of any kind are declared or implied. Readers acknowledge that the author is not engaged in the rendering of legal, financial, medical or professional advice. The content within this book has been derived from various sources. Please consult a licensed professional before attempting any techniques outlined in this book.

By reading this document, the reader agrees that under no circumstances is the author responsible for any losses, direct or indirect, that are incurred as a result of the use of the information contained within this document, including, but not limited to, errors, omissions, or inaccuracies.

Table of Contents

TABLE OF CONTENTS 3

INTRODUCTION 5
   WHAT WILL YOU GAIN FROM THIS BOOK? 11

CHAPTER 1 13

START WITH A MINDSET SHIFT 13
   THE WEALTH-BUILDING MINDSET 14
   MINDSET FOR DEBT-FREE LIVING 19
   FINANCIAL HELP FOR A SINGLE PARENT 21

CHAPTER 2 25

DEFINING YOUR FAMILY'S VALUES 25
   MAINTAINING FOCUS ON FAMILY GOALS 27
   STRENGTHENING FAMILY RELATIONSHIPS 30

CHAPTER 3 38

BUILDING A BUDGET FOR YOUR FAMILY 38
   DEFINE YOUR FINANCIAL VALUES 39
   HOW TO BUDGET AS A FAMILY 45
   PERFORMING A SPENDING AUDIT 48
   SETTING FINANCIAL GOALS FOR YOUR FAMILY 52
   USING TECHNOLOGY TO HELP YOU BUDGET 72
      Best Budgeting Software 74

CHAPTER 4 80

HOW TO ELIMINATE DEBT AND WHY IT'S SO IMPORTANT TO DO SO ... 80
   DO YOU HAVE TO BORROW TO INCUR DEBT? 81
   WHY IT'S IMPORTANT TO GET RID OF YOUR DEBT 82
   CREDIT CARDS ARE CONVENIENT BUT BE CAUTIOUS 93
      Understanding Credit Cards 94
      The Dangers of Credit Card Debt and How to Avoid Them 98

CHAPTER 5 103
EFFECTIVE METHODS TO BEGIN PAYING OFF YOUR DEBT 103

- THE AVALANCHE METHOD OF DEBT REPAYMENT 104
- THE SNOWBALL METHOD OF DEBT REPAYMENT 106
- OTHER STRATEGIES TO BEGIN REPAYING YOUR DEBT 108
- BRINGING DEBT INTO A MARRIAGE AND HOW TO DEAL WITH IT 114
- HOW TO TEACH CHILDREN ABOUT FINANCES AND DEBT 117

CHAPTER 6 125
SAVING MONEY FOR RAINY DAYS 125

- WHAT IS A RAINY DAY FUND? 125
- THE IMPORTANCE OF EMERGENCY FUNDS 131
- SINKING FUNDS: WHAT ARE THEY AND HOW DO THEY WORK? 135
  - *Why Do You Need a Sinking Fund?* *136*

CHAPTER 7 139
INVESTING IN YOUR FAMILY'S FUTURE 139

- TYPES OF INVESTMENTS 140
- COMPARING THE DIFFERENT TYPES OF INVESTMENTS 144
  - *Managing Investment Goals* *146*

CHAPTER 8 150
HOW TO RETIRE EARLY AND COMFORTABLY 150

- THE BENEFITS OF EARLY RETIREMENT 152
  - *Tips on Saving Money for Retirement* *154*

CHAPTER 9 156
HOW TO PRIORITIZE YOUR FINAL WISHES 156

- *The Modus Operandi of Life Insurance* *158*
- *Additional Benefits of Life Insurance* *161*
- WRITING YOUR LAST WILL AND TESTAMENT 162

CONCLUSION 165
REFERENCES 168

Introduction

You are standing in line for a coffee at your local cafe. You have to check your bank account app to see if you have enough room left on your overdraft to buy a mocha Frappuccino for yourself and a cream Frappuccino for your child. You might have to settle for just the beverage for your child. Your shoulders slump down as you sigh and wonder when things will get better. You get an email on your phone. It's the credit card company because you missed a payment last week. You wince while scrolling through the terms and conditions to determine the absolute minimum amount you need to pay to keep the bank off your back. If you are living life on the edge, then you are in the right place. And no, I don't mean living life on the edge in a fun and exciting way. The edge is a stressful and exhausting place to be. It consumes you with worry and anticipation, and it makes doing anything else really difficult. Have you ever tried bungee jumping? Living on the edge means that falling is all you are thinking about. Similarly, living a life encased in debt means that all you are thinking about is money and how you are going to scrape it together to buy a sub-par coffee and keep your savings afloat.

It's a feeling that starts in your chest and then seeps into every part of your existence. You can't pay rent, and you can't go out with your friends, you can't treat your partner to something nice, or get your child the toy they want. Everything, even buying groceries, feels like the biggest financial decision of your life. Your brain feels like a calculator as you make sums and try to guess where you might end up at the end of the month. You are exhausted—stuck in an endless loop of math sums and poor decisions. Where do you even begin? What does living a debt-free life even look like?

Many families are experiencing a similar situation with no end in sight. Unfortunately, there are many factors at play here—the economy, personal decisions, societal pressures, and bad planning are all responsible for the financial situation you find yourself in. Don't blame yourself. It has become increasingly difficult to support a household on the average family earnings of a standard North American family. Currently, the median household income is approximately $20,000 more than it was in the year 2000. However, increased inflation over the years means that proportionally, families were better off before the recession in 2008, even though they were earning less.

However, the inflation rate is not the only reason why the money earned is not enough to support a family. There is a strong relationship between debt and saving. Having debt makes it difficult to save. The odds may seem to be against you right now, but in this book, I will show you how to beat the odds and live a debt-free life. You may argue that it is impossible to pay off debt *and* save enough for you and your family. It isn't. The process will require some self-reflection and honest and realistic consideration of you and your family's needs and wants. What makes you happy? What is absolutely essential to your survival? From here, you can eliminate waste and focus on building your financial freedom.

In a situation where you are struggling with mounting debt and have no real savings, you probably feel like your options are limited. You may have many expenses to account for and limited resources. Most times, it's a battle between trying to provide for your family without constantly borrowing and trying to save for the future. If you are going to start your journey to financial freedom, you first have to understand why your current situation is not conducive to a stable and functioning financial situation. Here are some reasons why you might find building wealth and eliminating debt, particularly challenging:

1. **You don't earn enough money.** It is hard to save money when you are just trying to survive. How are you supposed to save and invest in assets if you barely have enough money to buy groceries at the end of the month without having to go into overdraft? Low-paying jobs, the absence of a side hustle, extended periods of unemployment, inadequate pay, and a lack of incentives in the workplace are all contributing factors to your less than desirable financial situation.

2. **You spend more than you earn.** It's simple math. If you have three apples and you want four, you are going to owe someone an apple at some point. If you have a low income, there may be times when you feel you have no other choice than to spend above your means. But if you are able to live comfortably within your means and still find yourself overspending, you may have to reconsider some of your financial choices. For instance, between 2017 and 2018, expenses on pets increased by 4.4%. The same goes for spending on entertainment, which went up to $3,226 per household in 2018 (Chapkanovska, 2020). Other nonessential items also experienced a boom. Living above your means is a surefire way to get yourself into debt. If you can't afford to have a pet, you shouldn't have one. In the famous words of the hip-hop artist Jay-Z, if you can't buy it twice, you can't afford it. Uncontrolled spending will affect your savings, make you borrow more than you

should, and ultimately place your family in a poor financial position.

3. **You don't have a budget or financial plan.** Keeping track of finances and expenditures can be time consuming. A budget is not like a New Year's resolution. You don't have to commit to exercising for the whole year, but you do need to commit to having a clear and concise financial plan. You don't go into work every day and keep track of your meetings and tasks in your head. You use a journal. Similarly, having a plan will help you avoid unnecessary spending while keeping track of your debt.

4. **You might not understand the basics of financial management.** You don't have to be a financial manager to be able to manage your funds, but you do need to have a general understanding of the basics. It can be difficult to know what to do with your money, how and where to invest, and making the wrong move can often lead to anxiety and pressure. Making a financial plan and understanding how you can make your money work for you will allow you to build your wealth exponentially. Did you know, parents are the primary source of financial management education for 44% of young adults? It is more than likely that if you lack the knowledge and skills to manage your family's finances, your kids will follow suit. So, keep reading and make sure your children don't fall into the same traps that you have.

5. **Speaking about money makes you uncomfortable.** Some societies find this to be a taboo topic; however, almost everyone in the world makes

money (or tries to, anyway). We live in a world that is centered around finances and economic wealth, so why wouldn't it be normal to talk about it? Speak about your finances and make sure you and your family are on the same page. Hiding this information will only make you feel scared and alone, and there really is no reason for that.

6. **Family dynamics.** Perhaps you are a single parent or have a stay-at-home partner and your family depends on one income. Maybe you are divorced, remarried and supporting two families all on your own. The structure of your family and your context might be a huge factor in your inability to save and live a debt-free life. In this case, you must take context into consideration and create a financial plan that benefits you and your situation.

What happens when you don't properly manage your family's finances? Since your finances are already in a grim condition, it's easy to believe your only option is to try and wing it. Unfortunately, that's not going to work. Neglecting to create a practical financial plan could lead to:

1. **Going into debt.** If you don't keep track of your finances, you might end up spending money unnecessarily or spending money you don't have. This is known as a vicious cycle. Once you start to spend money you don't have, you have to pay it back but to pay it back, you have to borrow more money until you are so consumed by debt you don't know whether you are coming or going. Sticking to a plan will help you make logical financial decisions and prevent falling into a debt trap.

2. **Unhealthy saving habits.** Without a financial plan, you are much less likely to intentionally save money. I know it can feel like a numbers game and that seems exhausting. But if you are making the right financial decisions and planning your spending, saving will become second nature.

3. **No investments.** If you aren't planning your finances properly, you probably won't be able to invest in anything because you won't have much left. Instead of planning for investments, you might spend the extra money on a new phone or television and find yourself wondering where all the money went. Planning is key in setting up a strong and stable financial future.

4. **Poor mental health.** Anxiety, depression, stress and sleeping disorders are all symptoms of living a busy and hectic modern life. Financial insecurity and not being in control of your finances can exacerbate stress. At the Money and Mental Health Policy Institute, Merlyn Holkar's research found that more than 1.5 million people across England suffer from both debilitating debt and mental health problems. 86% of the participants agreed that their financial situation worsened their mental health. Making a financial plan can help you lift yourself out of a bleak situation. Tailor the plan to your needs and abilities. Start slow and start small until you are strong enough.

5. **Family discord.** Unfortunately, the improper management of household finances may lead to a breakdown within the family unit. According to a poll by the Bank of Montreal, 68% of those surveyed say fighting over money would be their top reason for divorce. Communication is key when creating a financial

plan for your family. If you have a project at work, your boss doesn't hide the specifications of this project from you. This would make you unable to do your job and may build resentment. Similarly, hiding information from your family means they will be unable to play their part and contribute to a plan. Be honest, be frank, and get everyone on board.

In this book, I will show you how to avoid and unlearn these bad habits and practices. You *can* achieve financial success. No, you don't need a degree in accounting or financial management. This book will give you everything you need and more to be able to live a financially secure life.

What Will You Gain from This Book?

I hope that after reading this far in the book has already shown you that the life you want to live is not impossible. You can:

1. Change your mindset towards money.
2. Learn sound practices related to managing your family's finances.
3. Live debt-free and support your family without having to borrow.
4. Build wealth and improve your annual income.
5. Boost your savings, set up profitable investments and insurance for your family.

Don't get the wrong idea; taking back control of your financial life and experiencing sustainable growth in your household income is not going to be an easy process. About 17% of the American population faces financial struggles in most aspects of their lives and can't even afford to borrow. More than half struggle in some area of their financial lives and only 73 million people (19%) have healthy and active financial lives. Financial freedom and debt-free living require a conscious effort to do better. It won't always be easy, but it will be worth it.

This book contains a collection of money management techniques, tools, and recommendations that will help you on your journey to financial freedom. I recognize that there is no one-size-fits-all strategy that will work for all households. So, this guide contains proven best practices that have been distilled into actionable strategies, tips, and processes for any family. The book begins by stressing the importance of having a money mindset shift, defining family financial values and understanding family dynamics unique to your context and situation. From there, I will explore debt and credit management as these aspects of wealth building can make or break you.

Another essential element to financial security is saving money. How do you save on a tight budget? What do you do with your savings? This book will provide you with the how, what, and why of financial planning and saving. Having emergency funds can change your life. If you are worried about saving for a rainy day, look no further. But before you get into the nitty-gritty aspects of financial management, let's have a look at your life, your needs, and your expectations. Building a strong foundation is the key to achieving a financially secure life.

Chapter 1

Start with a Mindset Shift

"You become what you think about."

—Earl Nightingale

The first step of this process is to change your attitude towards money. You are probably here because of a few questionable financial decisions that have made you feel anxious and worried about your financial future and security. In order to be successful in this journey, you have to figure out what your relationship is with money and how you need to change it. Remember, this perception change is not only intended for you and your partner. Try to lay out a plan of action for your children and the people in your household. The journey to financial freedom can be complex, so wait until you are confident and secure in your outlook until you pass knowledge on to your family. Most of the things you will learn about building wealth, achieving financial success, and living debt-free begin within the mind. You learned more than half of what you already know about money at home. While your spending habits may have some generational influence, research shows that 84% of young people eventually experience better financial conditions than their parents.

The main focus of financial education is to reprogram your perception of money in a way that benefits you. If you respond to money and financial situations in the same way as your parents did, you may face a lot of difficulty in a modern context. The baby boomer generation was able to buy assets like a car and a house and send their kids to college and still have some money left to save. If you are a millennial, though, and you start buying assets, you might find yourself in deep debt for a very long time. The way we spend money changes constantly due to inflation rates, changing economic situations, and progressive social dynamics. This is why adapting your mindset is important. Times are changing and if you spend money the way your parents and grandparents did, you likely won't be very successful or financially stable.

There are timeless financial strategies that always win. But learning them usually requires a shift in money mentality. In this chapter, you will learn how to build the right money mindset and change old habits by reprogramming your mind.

The Wealth-Building Mindset

When you consider the rising amount of credit card debt in the world, you can start to appreciate why it is essential to develop a wealth-building mindset. Up to 90% of American families can barely survive on the income from their paycheck and they come out of the month with little to no savings.

So, what is a money mindset? Your beliefs about wealth creation, the way you perceive money, your opinions of financial conditions, and your attitude towards every aspect of financial management make up your money mindset. Defining what *wealth* means to you means that you have to consider economic conditions, personal aspirations, and current financial environments. To that end, five people picked at random would have five different amounts that define wealth for them. So, to someone who has a low income, $5000 might be an obscenely large amount of money. However, someone who earns a much higher salary might think that $5000 is but a drop in the ocean. Your definition of wealth contributes to and is also indicative of your money mindset. However, no matter your definition of wealth, one thing is constant—to create wealth, you must develop a mindset that allows you to:

- Set achievable and SMART money goals
- Spend wisely
- Plan for multiple streams of income
- Build up your savings; and
- Strategically invest in the right tools.

Contrary to what many people may think, these facets and goals are all equally important in your journey to financial freedom. Building up your savings is impossible without a strategic spending lifestyle. If you practice the best investment strategies without a goal that guides you on how to manage your earnings, you might wonder why you aren't saving as much. To get where you are going, you have to know where you are and vice versa.

Developing A Wealth-Building Mindset In 5 Steps

Committing to changing your relationship with money is a big step. However, taking conscious action and being intentional about changing your family's financial trajectory is monumental. If you are unsure of where to start and how to even begin changing the way you think about money, follow this five-step process:

Step 1: Set money goals

Building wealth takes time. But more than that, it requires purpose and direction. If you have no goals, financial motivation, or aspirations, then you won't have a wealthy mindset. You have to know where you want to go in order to get there. So, be sensible, be realistic, and start figuring out what you want. Do you want to become a millionaire? Do you want to start your own business and become independently wealthy? What about saving for college? If you don't have a reason to save, ask yourself what you would do if you didn't have any money? Even if you don't have a specific reason for saving, things can go wrong, people get sick, things break down, and you need to have savings to prevent these unfortunate events from compromising you financially.

Break up your goals into bite-size pieces so that you can effectively reach them. You aren't going to make one million dollars in a week unless you win the lottery. So, set realistic goals and give yourself a realistic timeframe. If the goal is too big, you might find yourself feeling discouraged and unmotivated. Smaller, quick goals that are easy to accomplish will give you the energy and motivation you need to fulfill your long-term and short-term money goals.

Step 2: Implement a budget

Budgeting is your best bet for spending less. A lot of people set up budgets to combat unnecessary expenditures in the family. The problem is always sticking to the budget. Be intentional when you set your budget. It's kind of like a New Year's resolution. You promise that you are going to work out every day for two hours and only eat raw vegetables and become an environmental warrior. These are all valiant resolutions and if you manage it, well done. However, the chances are that you didn't, and now you feel disappointed. Similarly, if you try to live so far below your means that you end up eating cereal and fighting over the last drop of milk, then you probably won't keep to the budget for very long. Keeping your goals realistic and manageable means sticking to the budget will be a lot more pleasant than it sounds.

Specify the essential needs of the family and list them in order of importance. Strikeout expenses that you can do without. Combine similar projects and save money when you do them together. Leave larger expenses for later and settle it as a long-term project by saving towards it. The point of budgeting is to take control of your spending, make better financial decisions, and live a responsible debt-free lifestyle.

Step 3: Invest strategically

Simple investment options allow your money to grow while you work and focus on making the income you need for running your daily life. Banking tools like interest-earning deposits are used by the wealthy to grow their money. Allowing your accounts to sit for longer earns you more money due to interest. Interest is the money charged for borrowing. If someone lends you money, you will have to pay the amount back plus interest. So why do you get interest on your savings account? Well, the banks use the money you deposit to lend to other people. Effectively, banks are borrowing from you and then paying you back the amount they borrowed plus interest. However, you always have the amount you deposited in your account. Don't worry about losing it.

Investing is a fundamental aspect of wealth-building. Even if you are a business owner, profit from sales is not enough to satisfy your financial aspirations. Take simple steps to put your money into the best and most profitable products in the stock exchange and watch your wealth build-up. Understanding the investment process doesn't happen in one day. Ask for help from a specialist or take a few classes. The internet is a bottomless source of knowledge and information, and it's basically free. If you don't want to go through the hassle and you have some money to spare, hire an investment manager. It will cost you a commission, but the gain from a successful strategy makes it worthwhile. You could also shadow successful investment managers and billionaire investors. Make your investment moves based on their most profitable strategies. That way, when they win, you do too.

Making the right investment call requires a wealthy mindset, the courage to take sensible risks, and the patience to apply common sense in picking the right commodity to invest in every time. Investments, when done successfully, are a good source of income because they can provide everything your family might want, secure the future, and account for emergencies.

Step 4: Supplement your income

If you have some extra time on the weekends, why not lend your skills and time to make some money on the side. If you don't have other interests and talents, then you could find side-hustles to supplement your income. Perhaps you are artistic and can make things and sell them to people. If you have services to offer, advertise them, and make a few extra bucks in the free time you have. Teach your children about business and the economy by showing them how to open a lemonade stand or sell the things they make. There are so many ways to sell your time, skills, and expertise outside of a full-time job. You just have to decide what you want to do, and do it!

You can save some money by using DIY (do-it-yourself) processes for some easy tasks instead of hiring a professional. In this way, you can learn a new skill and save some money. It might not seem like a lot, but before you know it, you may have fully funded your vacation with the supplemented income.

Step 5: Maintain focus

Your journey to achieving your financial goal is not going to be complete with a one-time, life-changing deal or investment move. That only happens in the movies. You must continue to focus on your goal and make an effort to reach it. Set out milestones to track your progress. In investing, some of your moves may not pay off. Don't despair. Be positive and focus on your next move. Learning and applying these steps will take a lot of focus and determination, but with the right foundation, you will find yourself in the money-making mindset in no time.

Mindset for Debt-Free Living

Having a money-making mindset and a debt-free mindset are similar but not quite the same. A wealthy mindset requires you to make more money and invest smartly with that goal in mind. A debt-free mindset requires you to spend and borrow less. In reality, you would need to live debt-free before you consider other aspects of wealth-building. One aspect that is similar in both wealth-building and debt-free living is that you need to define your goal. In this case, your goal is to manage your family income without any debt and without borrowing.

- **The most important aspect of debt-free living is to rethink the way you spend.** Be frugal with your expenses. Prioritize your needs and take care of the most important expenses, which will most likely be food, mortgage, utilities, and transportation. If you already have debt then living below your means will be necessary to start your journey to living a debt-free life. If you don't have debt, then you will still benefit from living below your means but your approach needn't be as intense as the former. When it comes down to it, you still want to be able to enjoy your life. You won't have to give up all the pleasures you have in life, but you will have to sacrifice some of them, if only until you are living confidently and debt-free.

- **Credit cards will not save you.** It is not a magic card that gives you free money. Sometimes credit can help you if you use it wisely and cautiously but try to avoid it at all costs. It can be too tempting to spend that money and before you know it you are knee-deep in debt.

- **Self-control and discipline are important in creating a debt-free lifestyle.** Be in charge of how you spend and what you spend your money on. Don't use money as a crutch or solution for your problems. This can be dangerous and leave you unable to find meaning in life. Instant gratification will leave you in an endless loop of buying. Practice delayed gratification and think about your purchases before you make them. Do you really need that $1000 spice holder when you have a perfectly good drawer at home? Cut down on how much you spend on nonessential items like entertainment and alcohol. Be courageous in your chosen lifestyle and stick with it until you achieve your goal.

- **Save, invest, and settle long-term debt.** While you work on paying off old debt, avoid taking on new debt. Don't fall into the vicious cycle of paying off your debt with borrowed money. The interest on these debts alone will be enough to make you feel hopeless.

- **Be able to say no and say it boldly.** If you are faced with a financial challenge and it seems like the only way out is credit, say no. Having the discipline to say no boosts your self-control and helps you to correct unhealthy habits.

- **Credit cards are not necessary for your family to survive.** You don't have to go all out on Halloween decorations or spend hundreds of dollars on Christmas lights. For people aged 35 and younger, 20% of their debt is due to credit cards and 21% due to student loans (Fay, 2020). In 2018, 40% of monthly incomes were spent on nonessential needs like clothes and entertainment. Make the right decisions and prioritize before making any big or unnecessary purchases.

Essentially, to live debt-free, you must define your unique core values. For some families, it will be easier to achieve debt-free living. For families that are so broke they are unable to get credit, financial freedom will be more challenging, but still not impossible. You just have to persevere and keep your intentions in-check at all times.

Financial Help for A Single Parent

Do single-parent families have the same opportunities as a two-parent household family does to become financially secure? If yes, what would you need to do differently? Is it demonstrably easier or harder to achieve financial success as a single parent? What conditions would make it so? As a single parent, there are other factors that need to be taken into consideration when working towards building wealth. As a single parent, you may find yourself in a situation where you feel the odds are stacked against you, and there is just no winning. In 2015, *The Guardian* reported that arrears owed by single-parent families in 2014 were up by 105% in comparison to the statistics in 2012. Families managed by single parents are more likely to owe rent and arrears on bills than two-parent families. It can be stressful having to balance work and family as well as working towards having strong financial goals. It may feel impossible, but there is hope. If you are a single parent, you might benefit from these financial options.

1. Consider filing for child support.

Yes, this is definitely an obvious one. Child support funds can go a long way towards providing for your family. Child support regulation and enforcement focus on making things easier for single parents managing families alone. Once you file the paperwork to initiate the process, the social services department in charge of child support will offer you the relevant services up to the point where you receive payments at the specified time. They can open up a case once you file the paperwork, locate the other parent, establish parentage, set up a child support order, set up payment, enforce order, and review it periodically to ensure compliance. Child support should take care of the necessities and help you reduce monthly payments.

2. Consider getting a higher-paying job.

Sticking to a job just for financial safety could be indicative of an ineffective money mindset. Once you know you have other options and you have the confidence to take charge of those options, you should get the job you deserve. Always be bold enough to know when a situation is not working and adapt to the situation. Consider leveraging your talent or learned skills to break into a higher-paying profession or finding a mentorship or paid internship program. You will be able to learn a new skill and better support your family.

3. Consider going back to school.

When you reevaluate the situation, you might find that you feel passionately enough about a subject to study it. Many institutions offer night classes and while this might make your life more challenging in the short-run, in the long run you will be able to get your dream job and better support your family. Going back to school, especially with a family to take care of, may seem scary. But, if you weigh the long-term gains to you, your family, and your sense of achievement, you may move from considering it to planning for it. The goal is to give yourself and your family a better chance to build generational wealth. Living a debt-free and financially secure life is not only about planning for the immediate future. It could take a significant amount of time to pay off outstanding debt, so you might as well pay it off doing something you love and that will give you more financial security.

4. Reconsider your housing options.

If living alone with your family and paying for a mortgage or rent is no longer an option, consider other living arrangements. House-share options are on the rise because many people can't afford to live alone anymore. Splitting the rent is like carpooling, but for your house. Also, if the option is available, consider moving back in with your family temporarily. You could work longer or start studying if your family can help you take care of your child. If these are not options for you, consider moving into a smaller home or a rental apartment to reduce your overall monthly spending.

5. Consider supplementary sources of income.

Remember, being in control of your finances is about managing your spending. Use part-time side hustles, a second job, or overtime to increase your monthly income and aid in your ability to pay off debt and start saving. Splitting your expenses with a family member could help reduce your monthly payments.

Try not to have preconceived assumptions of what is or is not possible. Remember, we are trying to *change* your mindset. Every option is a possibility and every door is open to you; you just have to know which one is the right door for you. While it might feel like debt is holding you back, remember to be positive and continue to dream. Set goals and define your aspirations. Ditch that ineffective money mindset and embrace a brighter outlook for the future.

Chapter 2

Defining Your Family's Values

"Don't tell me what you value. Show me your budget, and I'll tell you what you value."

—Joe Biden

In her book, *Traits of a Healthy Family* (1985), family life specialist Dolores Curran lists 56 characteristics of a healthy and functional family. Out of the 56, she ranks family values as the 7th most valuable trait necessary in sustaining a healthy household.

In this way, your financial freedom is your family's financial freedom. Everyone has a different way of doing things, a different structure, different values. Think of your family values like a car. Some people need to travel long distances for work and, therefore, need a car that is energy-efficient and able to withstand long journeys. Other people need more space because they have children and require a more practical means of transportation. Each and every individual and family has their own unique way of doing things that are specifically tailored to them. To better understand how, why, and what you need and want to spend your money on, you have to analyze your life and determine what your "family values" are as a unit. Your family, as a team has to identify and agree on your priorities and goals. So, setting up a good foundation for the future, changing your money mindset, defining values, and identifying your context are the first steps.

Family Values and Decision-Making

Apart from establishing sound financial management principles for your family, there are other reasons why a clear set of family values is invaluable. Firstly, set values help to develop a strong compass for your family. Values are especially useful when faced with difficult choices. Making financial decisions about important aspects of your family life can be challenging. You don't do it on a whim, without a plan or adequate information and help. Therefore, as in every aspect of your life, clearly defining what is most important to your family unit is the easiest way to set out a guideline or template for making difficult decisions. More so, it enables you to involve your partner and all members of your family in decisions and allows you to account for their interests and desires when setting goals or making decisions.

Family values or priorities should guide your household decisions around money. Understanding where you stand and where you want to go as a family unit will make keeping track of your goals and progress far easier. Maybe your career is just starting and you have to save money to send your kids to college one day. Your family values will be a lot different from someone who just graduated from college and is only financially responsible for themselves. Do you have an athletic family that competes in sports or are you more travel lovers? Do you have a more close-knit family or do you tend to be more distant? These kinds of questions will allow you to determine the values and traditions of family life that are important to you and will also guide you in your future decisions. For instance, if you establish eating healthy as one of your core family values, then having a line item in your family's budget for fast food take out wouldn't make the most sense.

Family Values and Relationships

The second aspect of family life in which having a defined value system is useful is in the way it affects the relationship between the members of your family. The priorities you set for your family define the dynamics of your relationship with your partner and children. According to Curran (1985), values are personal. On Curran's list of traits of a healthy family, developing trust is ranked fourth. The implication of this is that everyone in the family will have a similar value structure and this will allow the counterparts of the family to develop a level of trust with one another. Also, trust is a value that can be defined, taught, and maintained. Relationships between partners may deteriorate when family values that help them build trust are not nurtured. Make sure you have each other's best interests at heart when defining family values. You can't build a sturdy house on an unstable foundation.

Maintaining Focus on Family Goals

Values serve as guidelines. Just like grandma's cookbook with the family's favorite recipes—a family's core values act as a map and compass that keeps everyone on the right path towards achieving the goals that have been set. If you are worried about how you and your family unit will maintain and consciously live by these values, you will have to make sure that everyone is on the same page. If one of the priorities only serves to benefit a small portion of the family, why should everyone adhere to them? Make sure the values that you set up serve a purpose for every individual in the family unit.

Let's say you want to move your entire family to a different neighborhood in a good school district by the time your newborn baby turns two. To do that, you will need the other kids to accept more responsibility on behalf of the family so you can work longer hours at work. Perhaps they can help with starting dinner preparation or taking on other household duties. Remember, you are not alone as parents. Your family can help you and if you clearly define your financial goals and what they can mean to your family, building financial wealth will truly be a team effort. It is easier to achieve the family's goals when everyone is guided by similar values. In times of difficulty, strong family priorities are crucial. They allow you to remain grounded and focused on the goals and outcomes of the family unit.

Family Values and Money

Your family dynamics will determine how you manage household finances. Family values will allow you to determine how you want to live and how you should proceed to make those desires a reality. Identifying your family values is a strategic step in creating the right environment for building wealth. Family values define your family's lifestyle, particularly its structure, dynamics, the roles and functions of its members, its beliefs, social ideals, aspirations, and outlook for the future.

Values can be non-traditional, traditional or cultural. Trends often start in the family and are passed down through multiple generations. Families headed by millennials may base the better part of their family values on a combination of evolutionary proofs and desires. However, no new family is ever free of pre-existing beliefs and principles. You just have to decide which beliefs add value to the family unit and which don't. If you are a millennial, you may value the environment more than your parents did. In this way, reducing waste and buying ethically sourced and local products may be a priority to your family. You can decide what is important to you and make financial decisions with that in mind. Here are some values that will affect your family finances in positive ways:

- **Diligence and hard work** are positive values. They push you to get what you want and make a better life for you and your family.

- **Commitment and devotion** signify dedication to your family's welfare and growth. Dedication to your goals and aspirations helps you focus on the aspects of your life that are the most important to you.

- **Frugality, discipline, and self-control** are qualities of moderation. They enable you to spend wisely, set up and keep to a budget, and manage your money wisely.

- **Respect, loyalty, faithfulness, and trust** help to build stable and well-balanced relationships within the family.

- **Responsibility** gives you a sense of duty—to yourself and your family. Responsibility also helps you and your partner to distinguish your functions as best as possible.

Money and Relationships

In a family unit, the lifestyle of its members, the relationship between spouses or partners and their children, and cooperation among all of these aspects are valuable in building the right mindset for effective household financial management. In North America, money issues are the top causes of problems faced by most families. Money issues can often lead to family dysfunction, distrust among partners, and mental health issues. Yet, only 20% of spouses discuss financial matters with their partners before they marry. Keeping your finances a secret with the people whom you spend most of your time with, and have committed to, could be more damaging than helpful in most instances. Yes, you should always protect your best interest but you can be smart about your money and still communicate openly about it.

In 2011, the lifestyle magazine *The Week* published that 31% of married people who combine their finances lie to their spouses about money. The breakdown of that number shows that more than half of them have at one-point hidden cash from their partners, and up to 15% had a secret bank account. The report further showed that 11% of these people lied about the debt they owed, and another 11% have lied about their income. Hiding money, even if it is a trust fund for your children, is not the best way to develop a relationship with your partner. Secrets and poor communication create fissures in familial relations and if you add financial problems to the mix, you might find yourself in a stressful situation.

Strengthening Family Relationships

There are simple ways to improve your relationship with your partner and the rest of your family. But, building closeness and togetherness is a lot easier if everyone is on the same page and has the same values. Therefore, I will provide you with a 6-step approach to setting and maintaining specific values for your family. This approach can bring you closer to your partner and children and ultimately improve your relationship with your family.

In situations where relationships deteriorate, especially due to money problems, a solution may seem impossible to find. If this happens, focus on the things that connect you to your partner. If you are struggling to get yourself out of a particular mindset, seeking professional counseling might be worth considering. The effect of negative spousal relationships on the family goes beyond financial repercussions. These tensions can also affect a child's physical and mental health. Saving, investing, budgeting, and growing wealth means nothing if the process breaks up your family or affects your children negatively. Remember, there is more to life than money and remaining committed to changing toxic patterns and habits will help you and your family realize that. Take responsibility for your functions in the household. Be dedicated to the goal of making your lives and your children's future better.

Besides aiding in decision-making, relationships, and financial freedom, the values you define with your family will affect their discipline and ethics. We have all grown up in a world with different ethical values and expectations. We all have varying values and opinions. Find principles that are specific to you and your family and create a healthy environment for everyone involved. Exploring good values will also benefit how you and your family view money. Perhaps instant gratification and material wealth won't matter as much if you have a strong and supportive community. Identifying your values will help you live within your means and stops you from wanting more than you need. One of the main causes of loss of family wealth is extravagant lifestyles. Try living within your means and focusing on self-improvement instead of trying to impress the world with your physical possessions.

Family values play a central role in your family's goal of living debt-free, growing and maintaining generational wealth, and gaining financial freedom. The question then is; when is the perfect time to define the values that will guide your family through it all?

When Should You Set Family Values?

Set family values as early as possible. The purpose of this chapter is for you to realize that beyond mathematics, money management, debt-free living, and financial growth begins with the right attitude. Cultivating the right lifestyle early in the process is the only way to build this attitude. Developing a way to get your family focused on setting priorities and goals should be one of the first things you do going into the process. Planning a family with your partner or spouse should create the space you need to define the collective goals, values, and functions of each family member. So, don't wait to figure out what you want. Define your values now and start your journey to financial freedom. A plane can't fly if it only has wings. It needs a whole bunch of other parts before it can effectively accomplish the task of flying—and so do you. You can't just be debt-free. You have to engage with yourself and your family before that is possible.

Where to Begin?

There is no one-size-fits-all strategy or method for setting up family values and goals. What is most important is defining your fundamental beliefs in such a way that they resonate with you and your partner. To prepare for the 6-step strategy, there are three stages your plan must cover:

1. **Define.** This first step will involve you and your partner. You have to build your values on collective desires and qualities and also focus on eliminating the undesirable ones. If your spouse is an impulsive spender, you might want to consider adding self-control, discipline and delayed gratification to your family values.

   The point of setting values is not to get sidetracked in your mission of giving your family a good life. Therefore, the goals you want to achieve will determine the qualities you identify as your family's core values. The way to start is to list your goals and aspirations. Make sure your goals are time-sensitive as this will help you measure your progress and the extent to which you have maintained the family values.

2. **Teach.** Passing down these values to your children can take many forms. Sometimes through conversations, through observation or even corrective actions. The most effective way, however, is by example. Teach your kids good values by being the best representation of these goals. Teach your children trust, love, and loyalty by expressing it with your partner. Teach them frugality by avoiding extravagant spending. Show them how you came to make your decisions and give them the opportunity to learn useful and effective skills from you.

3. **Maintain.** This is where it gets challenging. Sometimes it is hard to be the perfect representation of the family values you set out. Sometimes you make mistakes or fall back into old habits. That's okay; just remember to get back to those core values. Maintaining the family's values is a daily test. Prioritize your goals and make sure your decisions serve them.

Stick to your values, try not to get distracted, remain focused on your goals, and keep trying. Some days will be more difficult than others. Remind yourself why you want financial freedom and to live a debt-free life. Soon, you and your family will be able to live a life in which these values are inherent and fully integrated into your collective lifestyles. It will be like breathing. You don't notice you are doing it but it is actually keeping you alive.

Getting Your Family Onboard

When setting and maintaining the family values, it is important that you and your partner approach the situation with a gentle, kind, and accepting attitude. Forcing your children to abide by certain rules and beliefs will take away their autonomy and personal freedom. Make sure you use this space to consult them and understand what they need and want from the situation.

Once you have come to a unanimous decision regarding the family values and core beliefs, these actions can begin to take the form of habits as you integrate them into your lifestyle. The process is supposed to be organic and holistic. Use it as an opportunity to learn more about your family. This process will lead to the right money mindset needed for creating wealth and living debt-free. These six steps will help you get your family on board and keep everyone focused on the collective goals and aspirations of the family.

Step 1: Communicate!

Talk it out. Use descriptive words to communicate your definitions of values. Create opportunities that give you time to talk to your family about aspects that concern and affect them. As much as you need to speak, you also need to listen. Being a good listener goes beyond hearing what is being said. Create a space and environment in which your children can be comfortable enough to talk to you. Create a judgment-free zone. They won't always want what you want or be who you want them to be but they are your children and they should be supported and loved by you no matter what. Don't just listen to what they are saying; listen to what they aren't saying. Observe their reactions and tiny changes in their behavioral habits. By doing this you can anticipate what is going on in their lives and provide the necessary support and guidance.

Communication is also valuable to your relationship with your partner. When it comes to handling family matters, the "don't talk" approach simply does not work. Apart from the fact that it may leave you feeling estranged from your partner, you might also feel the crushing pressure of trying to carry everything on your own. If the family's income is in danger, communicate that to them. Let the kids know that tighter budgets are the best way forward. Help them understand why you must prioritize saving. Poor communication can intensify money problems, leaving you worse off than when you started.

Step 2: Spend time together

Try to slow down and make sure you spend some time with your family. If you as a parent, focus more on working and providing financially, other aspects of family life may suffer. Not only will you miss pivotal moments in your partner's or children's lives, but it can be difficult to pass on good values if you never see one another. Take a break once in a while to spend time with your kids, attend soccer and baseball games, dance recitals, or eat dinner together. Make sure you are present for each other. Obviously, you don't need to stop working to spend time with your family. I doubt that would solve your financial issues. However, it does mean that when you do spend time with your family, you should be engaged and mindful. This step allows you to find the time to communicate with your family. It also gives your kids time to observe your life and reactions to conflicting values so they may learn from you.

Step 3: Be the example you want them to emulate

This goes without saying, but if you are going to be spending all that time with your family, you should make sure that you are setting a good example for them. They won't find any value in carefully laid out family values if you don't reflect them and act accordingly. Be conscious of what you do and say. Be sensitive and intentional in the way you teach them values. Do not force values on your children. Be the best version of yourself you can be. This will not only inspire the people around you but it will motivate you to keep living according to your value structure.

Step 4: Family rituals

If you are struggling to find time to spend as a family, start a ritual. Don't just make eating dinner together a one-off event. Implement it into your daily schedule. Make sure you go around the table and actually talk to each other. Prepare dinner together and offer support after a long day. This kind of structure can be comforting and will create a reliable space for the family to let loose in.

Maybe you don't have time to commit to a daily family dinner, send them daily messages, do something on the weekend, pick up a hobby together. Not only will you be learning a new skill, but you will also be learning it together, as a family. If you can financially plan together, you can spend meaningful quality time together. The two are not mutually exclusive. Understanding your family and yourself will make building wealth and living debt-free far easier.

Step 5: Involve them

When making family decisions, involve your family in a way that makes them feel like they are a central part of the decision-making team because, in reality, they are. You have a family; you have responsibilities and you should involve everyone as appropriate. Other people have opinions and valuable input they can contribute to the family. Create an inclusive and open space for idea sharing and communication.

Step 6: Be patient

Another way to show your kids how much you trust them is by letting them be responsible for aspects of family life. They may not get it right at first but, be patient and correct gently.

Practice giving your children more freedom, observe, and gradually expose them to different real-life scenarios. Help them understand how to react to negative values without compromising themselves. If you do it successfully within the household, they will understand how to respond when a similar situation arises.

Learning effective and useful values will also translate in their response to money matters. Teaching your children moderation and discipline will help you keep to your budget, save more, and even invest. A healthy and supportive family lends emotional support, improves general health, and sets the tone for financial success.

Chapter 3

Building a Budget for Your Family

"It's not your salary that makes you rich, it's your spending habits."

—Charles A. Jaffe

To help you manage your money effectively and stay out of debt you will need to establish and maintain a budget. You may have tried using a budget before and it wasn't effective. But you are reading this book for a reason so let's stick this out together. It is easy to underestimate how useful a budget can be. Think of it like organizing your kitchen. You don't just throw knives and spoons in the same drawer or put your pots in the fridge. If that were the case, you would struggle to find the equipment you need when cooking or eating. In the same way, you have laid out your house to bring you joy and make life easier. You put dining furniture in the dining room, your bed is in the bedroom and your shampoo is in the shower. Imagine having to go to the kitchen to fetch your shampoo every time you wanted to shower. This would take long and is simply impractical. Similarly, you can't just put your money in random places and expect everything to be fine. A budget will help you achieve your goals. Like I said, to get where you are going, you need a map. There is no point in following a map that has no structure or route. Therefore, your budget must be well-thought-out and planned in order to give you the best possible chance to pull yourself out of debt and into wealth building. One of the significant benefits of developing and sticking to a budget is that it is a skill you can pass down to your children. However, the first thing you need to do before creating a budget is to determine your family's financial values. You have decided how you want to proceed as a family and the kinds of priorities you want to base your lives on. Financial values are a little different. They deal with your financial context and the financial foundation you want to build in order to live a comfortable and stable life.

Define Your Financial Values

Financial values are the beliefs you and other members of your family have about money. These beliefs will differ from one individual to another, but you must create values that every member of your family can agree with and implement. Your financial values will permeate into various areas of your life, including income, debt, money management, spending, and saving. To determine your financial values, you need to ask yourself specific questions. Depending on the answers your financial values will become more apparent. However, you should first understand the importance of having clear financial values. There are three parts to defining your values, mainly why you need to define them, how to create them, and how to oversee these financial values.

1. **Why You Need to Define Your Financial Values**

- **They can influence your financial decisions through behavior.**

As an individual, your values often have a massive influence on your behavior. You might find that you fall into one of two categories. You could be someone who saves or someone who spends. Yes, there are many nuances and you might be a balance of both, but it is still useful to identify whether you relate to one more than the other. If you are inclined to save, then the financial decisions you make will put you in a healthy position. On the other hand, individuals who are inclined to spend will often find themselves in difficult financial situations. Since values are difficult to change, it is also difficult to turn a spender into a saver overnight.

Traits such as pessimism, procrastination, or even idleness can influence an individual or household's finances. A pessimist will only see the negative aspects of an investment, never taking time to assess the positives. Being idle takes away a chance to consider other opportunities to generate income. In this way, we're all different and value different aspects of life. Some people value working hard and others don't. However, understanding when your behaviors are harmful to your financial stability is the first step in addressing these negative financial habits and values.

- **They can influence your emotions.**

Humans are creatures of emotion. We aren't robots. So, when we make decisions, we tend to follow our emotions and feelings instead of listening to logic. However, when it comes to finances, it is best to limit the influence of your emotions on these decisions. This is more difficult to do than many people are willing to admit. As an example, say a friend asked you to invest in their new company. If you don't really have the money to spare then a decision like this could possibly put you in a deep financial hole. Another example could be choosing a financial advisor because you like them instead of choosing them for their expertise and skill level. And of course, we've all heard of retail therapy. Some people allow emotions such as frustration, boredom, sadness and anger to influence financial decisions.

- **They can impact your habits.**

The values you have will impact the habits you develop. These include your general habits and financial habits. These may be the values you developed as a child or those you develop as an adult. For example, individuals who place value on environmental protection often develop a desire to buy organic products and perhaps even become vegan later in life. In this way, the things you value will influence your habits and how you behave in life. If you value your safety, you might be more inclined to spend money on extra locks or a safer apartment. This is why identifying your family values was such an important step at the beginning of this process because, without a clear direction of how you want to act and what is important to you, you will struggle to get on the right path. The family values you have set out will also have a big impact on your financial values and creating a space for the two to work simultaneously and symbiotically will make building wealth and living a debt-free life easier.

2. How to Create Your Financial Values

As you go on to create financial values for your family, you must document these values. Formalizing them makes it easier for the family unit to internalize the values and implement them into daily life. To create financial values for your family, you can take a five-step approach:

i. Money Management

ii. Saving

iii. Spending

iv. Income

v. Debt

i. Money management

Money management refers to the system you have in place for monitoring the finances of your family. Making money management a financial priority will help you stay organized as a family unit. Much like making a budget, money management is about keeping track of everything you spend and earn. When figuring out how to manage your money, you should consider how you will track your finances and how you currently keep your finances organized. Do you just spend and earn and let the bank tell you when you are in the red? Or do you have a meticulous plan outlining expected incomes and expenses for the month? If you have the latter, you probably find that you have little debt and have already started building wealth toward your future. However, if you find that you struggle to manage your money, making a detailed plan will set you on the right track to a debt-free life.

If you are wondering how to track your finances, there are many methods and you will have to choose one that suits your lifestyle. You can use apps or your phone to keep track of your money management if you find this to be convenient. However, if you are more creative then you can set up a mind map or make a chart. This might be fun for your children to follow. Through regular monitoring and documentation of cash flow in the family, it is easy to know where and how every penny in the household is spent.

ii. Saving

Defining your family's saving culture will help you figure out how you want to save in the future. Maybe you want to save but you also have other hobbies and interests that require money. In this case, you can decide what is more valuable to you in the long-run. However, this does not mean that you can forgo saving. You still have to put money aside and make sure all of your debts are paid, but you can decide how much you want to save depending on your financial values. The questions you need to answer when analyzing this area include:

- What do you think about saving money?
- Are there specific savings strategies in your family?
- How do you approach saving when you have debt?
- Are you naturally thrifty or are you a big spender?

iii. Spending

How you spend money will allow you to create a useful and comprehensive budget and it will also help you figure out your spending philosophy as a family unit. If you enjoy thrifting and couponing, then your spending philosophy will spur you on to financial stability. However, if you spend money as quickly as you get it, this could be the reason for your debt. In this case, it is important to reevaluate your financial values. Here are some questions to help:

- Are you an impulsive spender?
- When do you spend money?
- Do you or members of your family consider yourselves to be spenders?
- Is there any noticeable weakness you have towards spending money?

iv. Income

Family income plays a crucial role in the financial health of the family. The higher the income to expenses ratio, the more surplus you will have at the end of the month. This will allow you to save and pay off your debt. However, not everyone has access to a six-figure salary and that makes financial stability a bit harder. Spending and income are closely linked because you likely have many expenses that you need to pay off in a month, and you do this with the money coming in. Here are some questions that can give you a better understanding of your income values:

- How much do you want to earn?
- What do you think of your earnings now?
- Why do you feel this way?

v. **Debt**

Many people believe that debt is almost unavoidable. Unless you have been set up with a trust fund or have a family to fall back on, you will most likely experience debt at some point in your life. Whether for small expenses like new shoes or large costs such as a house mortgage. That said, everyone's debt philosophy should be to avoid debt. However, it is worth identifying where you are in your life at the moment. Are you on the brink of retirement and still have to pay off your student loans? Have you just graduated from college and gotten into some credit card debt? Identifying where you are will make it easier to get where you want to be. To determine your values regarding debt, you need to answer these questions:

- Do you prioritize clearing your debt over other financial obligations?
- Are you willing to go into debt to get something you want?
- Do you take steps that encourage delayed consequences over delayed gratification?

- Are you comfortable having credit card balances?

3. Overview of Your Financial Values

The five-step approach is useful in helping you determine your financial values. When you complete this approach, you should have a list of these values–as well as a list of values that you want to change or pursue. Use this information and make an overview for yourself and your family so that you can stay on the right track. What can you get from an overview of your financial values? The overview is simply a document that you can use to categorize all of your values. For example, your values may indicate that you love discipline in your finances. Another individual may have values that indicate a focus on sustainability. Whatever your values are, they are important to you and should be nurtured and listened to. It is counterproductive to use a financial strategy or debt repayment method that goes against your core family and financial values.

How to Budget as a Family

A budget is an estimation of your spending and income. So, instead of just spending without any real thought, a budget tells you to spend a certain amount on food, a specific amount on rent etc. It is a form of money management, except the plan requires you to plan for the future. This can be a yearly budget or a weekly budget but the most popular and effective time frame to use is a monthly budget. This gives you an idea of how you spend your income, where you can cut down, and where you can afford to spend a little more. That being said, it is also useful to have a long-term budget to make sure you reach your financial goals like early retirement or sending your children to university. When creating a budget as a family, there are specific steps you can take to put you on the right track. In this section, you will learn about these steps to help you get started. The first thing you need to do is:

1. Get on the same page.

Your spending habits may differ, and so might your preferences, but even if they do, it is important to know these differences. If you and your partner are both saving and spending in different ways, consolidating your finances will be challenging. However, to make the budget function effectively, you must understand the need for compromise. For a budget to be effective, everyone must be willing to change their habits for the greater good. If half of your family is dedicated to saving but the other half spends more than you budgeted for, it will lead to conflict and an unstable financial situation.

2. Determine your income and expenses.

Before you start creating the budget, you need to know your current income and expenses. You can figure this out by reviewing your current financial situation. Look at your bank transactions to figure out what you spend your money on and how much you spend. The family income is easy to determine since it is a sum of everything each individual in the family earns. When determining the income of your family, honesty is crucial. If one partner is hiding the specifics of their income, it will be impossible to create a budget that works.

What are the things you spend on as a family? Do you eat out often? Do you purchase clothes and shoes monthly? You will incur many expenses as a family, so you need to identify all of them through an audit. Your bank statements and credit card statements are excellent sources of information regarding your expenses and income. A careful analysis of your income and expenses will give a clear picture of the family's current financial situation. Through this analysis, you will also determine the amount of money that mysteriously "disappears"–yes, it does happen. When you have money that disappears without being accounted for, it means there is a financial leak somewhere in your household. These are often a result of spending habits that need to change.

3. Analyze your debt.

A lack of proper financial planning will often lead you into debt. It doesn't matter if your family's income is enough to cover the expenses; your family may be in debt without a budget, financial goals, and adequate planning. When you identify how much debt the family has, the next step is to create a repayment plan. For this plan to work, you need to stop getting into more debt. There are different debt elimination strategies you can use, so pick one that works for your family. Also, figure out what debt you have. Is most of your debt coming from your credit card? Is it coming from the new car you bought? It will be counterproductive to address your car loan when the real problem may be your credit card debt.

4. Find ways to reduce your taxes.

If you spend a lot of money on your taxes, then it's time to find ways to reduce it. Effectively reducing your taxes creates more cash for you to save or redirect to debt repayment. You can start by opening a savings account with tax benefits. Also, if your family has a high-deductible health insurance plan, you can make a tax-exempt deduction, which you deposit into a health savings account.

5. Pick a budgeting tool.

Now that you have a clear picture of your expenses, debt, and income, you can pick a budgeting tool. This can be a paper tool or an electronic budgeting tool. I will discuss several apps and programs that are effective tools for budgeting at the end of this chapter.

Performing a Spending Audit

"The best way to save money is not to lose it."

—Les Williams

As a family, the state of your finances is a reflection of your spending. Therefore, you can improve your finances when you improve your spending habits. However, many families have limited information on their spending habits. This lack of information makes it difficult for you to change your financial situation. To help you overcome this issue, you must perform a spending audit. This is an audit in which you carefully analyze the spending behavior of your family members. Through this spending audit, you take your family spending out of autopilot mode and make spending a more deliberate and intentional action. This prevents you from spending more than you need to and makes it easier to follow a budget. By doing a spending audit, you can identify various expenses that are unnecessary in your family. So, how do you perform a spending audit?

1. Create time for the process.

Executing a spending audit isn't something that you can achieve in 30 minutes. It is a process that can take several hours. Don't let this discourage you. Once you have everything organized, it shouldn't take too long. If you need to organize your bills and create a budget, you may need to set aside an additional three or four hours for this process. Hence, you need to pick a day when you know you will have a lot of free time. But you can also move through this process incrementally. If you are busy, set aside 15 minutes a day to add to the audit, gather a bit of data every day and your audit will be done in no time!

2. Gather crucial data.

Just like a business audit, data is crucial in performing a family spending audit. The first place to get your data is from your current family budget. From here, you can move on to other sources like bank statements, bills, and credit card statements. The idea is to get information from any source that relates to your finances. This includes both your savings and expenses. Collecting data from the last 3-6 months will be helpful in this situation.

3. Assess your family financial goals.

Family financial goals are crucial to stabilizing your finances and building wealth. Without concrete goals, it is impossible to perform a high-quality spending audit. If you don't have financial goals, now is the right time to create them. In the next section, you will learn more about setting financial goals, including short-term and long-term goals, but for now, it is important to start thinking about what you would like in the future.

4. Create a list of your expenses.

This list should contain all of your regular monthly expenses. If you bought a car last month, then you might not want to include this in the list of expenses because it is not something you do every month. This list can then be subdivided into other categories, but remember to add other expenses specific to your family. The list of expenses should include, but are not limited to:

- Life insurance
- Internet bills
- Cell phone bills
- Mortgage/Rent
- Utilities
- Groceries
- Transportation
- Vehicle maintenance
- General insurance
- Clothing

5. Analyze each bill/expense.

Now that you have a list of all your expenses, it is time to analyze each of them. During your analysis, you must determine which bills are essential and which aren't. One thing you must note during this process is that the expenses that are vital to your family may not be necessary to other families. Create time to discuss with your spouse, and if your kids are old enough, involve them in the process. There are various actions you can take when analyzing each expense. One of these is to look for ways to cut down the amount you spend on expenses you want to keep. For example, you can find a cheaper phone or internet plan for your family. If you spend too much on snacks in your home, then it may be time to cut down on this expense or eliminate it. Another option is to switch to streaming services and cut off cable subscriptions in your home. There are many ways to downsize, but the most important part of this process is to identify where you are overspending.

6. Take advantage of deals and discounts.

This is just one way to be more conscious of your spending. There are periods when certain items will go on sale at your local grocery store and you should take advantage of those sales. Start taking note of these periods and using them to your advantage. This idea isn't limited to your groceries. You can also get deals on your insurance and other essential expenses.

7. Don't rush into making decisions.

When performing a spending audit, don't rush it. Although some expenses may not be in your best interest, it is usually unwise to immediately get rid of them. An example will be getting rid of a car. Paying off a car loan is usually drawn-out and expensive, but trying to get rid of the vehicle as soon as possible isn't always the best option. In such instances, make sure you get as much information regarding the process as you can. What will it cost you to get rid of it? What will it cost you to keep it? Which option is the best? You don't want to end up selling the car for less than it is worth and still come out of the situation with debt to pay on a car that you don't even own anymore. Giving yourself a due date by which you must decide will also help you take this process seriously.

8. Make the most of your free cash.

One of the most crucial steps in building wealth and gaining financial freedom is to make your money work for you. As you perform your spending audit, you cut down on unnecessary expenses and end up with surplus cash. This extra cash is what many people will decide to put into a savings account. This is where you need to make a wise decision. The best option is to invest your extra cash into other profitable sources. Some individuals will argue that a savings account generates interest for you, but in reality, these accounts aren't as profitable as many other options available. You can start by learning the basics of investing—if you don't have this knowledge already. For example, you can invest in stocks, bonds and real estate as a start. Finding an investment option that works for you is what matters. As you begin to educate yourself on various investment options, you also improve your ability to handle money as an individual and family unit.

Setting Financial Goals for Your Family

"Financial freedom is available to those who learn about it and work for it."

—Robert Kiyosaki

In its simplest form, a financial goal is any plan you have for your money. What plan do you have for your money as a family? Does this plan include setting aside money to build a college fund? A financial goal can be a short-term or long-term goal. An example of a short-term financial goal is a monthly budget. These are goals that will help you actualize your long-term goals. Some long-term financial goals include building a college fund and saving for retirement. Imagine Olympian and athlete Usain Bolt decided to start training for the 100m sprint without setting a goal for himself. Do you think he would have broken the world record if this was the case? Yes, he is fast, but pushing himself toward that goal made the impossible possible. Goals can motivate you when you are in the final stretch of your journey and without them, you might give up a few meters before the finish line. The main reason you need financial goals is to give you something to work towards. Without a focus as a family, it is easier to spend without worrying about the adverse effects of your financial habits. When you have financial goals, you will have money available for the things that matter, when you need it the most. This includes having enough money to send your kids to post-secondary school or live the lifestyle you desire after retirement. Setting goals for your future is the next step of financial planning and wealth building.

1. How to set financial goals.

There are different steps you can take when setting financial goals. However, the best financial goal is a SMART goal. What does this mean? In this section, you will find out what SMART goals are and why they are essential in your journey. Nonetheless, you still need to prioritize your needs and differentiate your goals before you can set out SMART goals for financial planning and stability.

Prioritize your needs

Learning to prioritize is essential in all areas of your life. Prioritization helps you manage your limited time and resources effectively to help you achieve the things that matter most. In creating financial goals, you must create a list of your goals and then prioritize this list. If living an environmentally conscious life is important to you, then you need to incorporate this into your set of goals. If you need to send your kids to college, then this will be a goal that you need and want to achieve.

Separate the short-term from the long-term

The goals you set will undoubtedly need to be achieved within the short-term or long-term. Separating your goals into these categories will make it easier for you to work towards them.

Short-term goals are goals that can be completed within a year. Mostly they relate to your desires for the coming days, weeks, and months. A long-term goal requires you to plan ahead a bit more. The goals will most likely be five to ten-year plans. It is important to note that your short-term goals should complement the long-term goals as you will inevitably be working through them to achieve long-term financial stability. Also, once you have set your goals, that isn't the end of it. You have to continuously update and rework your goals to fit into your changing lifestyle. Perhaps what you thought you wanted ten years ago is not the same as what you want now. Perhaps you can push yourself to save a bit more than you have been. Keep updating your goals to make sure you stay motivated and put yourself on the fast track to a financially secure and debt-free life.

2. Set up SMART goals.

SMART is an acronym that helps you plan your goals. It stands for:

- S–Specific
- M–Measurable
- A–Attainable/Achievable
- R–Realistic
- T–Timely/Timebound

SMART Goals are Specific.

When setting a financial goal, make sure your goal is specific. What this implies is that the goal must not be generalized. For example, if your goal is to save more money, writing it down as *I need to save $5,000* is more specific and easier to work towards. Overgeneralizing your goals can make them feel vague and unreachable. If you are specific about your goals then you know exactly what you want to achieve and how you are going to get there. You don't go to a restaurant and ask for "chicken." The waiter would probably be confused and ask you to be more specific. Similarly, understanding your goals will get you what you want.

SMART Goals are Measurable.

An excellent financial goal is one you can measure to determine if you are making progress or not. As in the previous example, working towards a specific amount will keep you motivated and allow you to see your progress first-hand. If your goal is $5000 and you have $4,000, then you know you are only $1,000 away from achieving your goal. However, if you have a general goal to save more money, it won't matter if you have $1,000 or $10,000 in your account since there is no specific target to compare it to.

SMART Goals are Achievable.

When setting goals, you shouldn't set goals that you can't achieve. This defeats the purpose of setting goals and it can be demoralizing. An achievable goal makes you more creative in your steps towards attaining it. To set an achievable goal, you must first assess the resources at your disposal. If you manage these resources effectively, you will be able to achieve your goal. Another way to determine an achievable goal is to identify other individuals that have achieved it. If there are others who have completed a similar goal, then it isn't beyond your reach. Despite a goal being challenging, you must be able to achieve it; otherwise, you will probably fail, and it will be harder to pick yourself back up again.

SMART Goals are Realistic.

For a goal to be realistic, it must be achievable within a given timeframe, using the resources available to you. Consider a household with a monthly income of $10,000 and monthly expenses of $7,000. If the household's financial goal is to build a savings of $30,000 in five months, this goal is unrealistic. Considering the resources available, it is possible to create a savings of $30,000. However, the timeframe makes it impossible. Assuming the $3,000 left after paying for the monthly expenses is free cash, a savings of $30,000 is achievable in 10 months. Therefore, any time frame shorter than ten months makes the goal unrealistic. In determining a realistic goal, it is essential to assess your commitment and the commitment of other family members in achieving the goal. Is your spouse willing to cut down on some of their expenses to meet the goal? Are your kids ready to give up some of the fun activities they have gotten used to? Any goal that you set without getting other family members' commitment will be impossible to achieve, thus, making it unrealistic.

SMART Goals are Timely.

For a goal to be timely, it means the goal must have a timeframe. The timeframe of a financial goal is what helps you determine if it is a short-term or long-term goal. If there is no time constraint on a goal, then it will be challenging to get enough motivation to achieve it. If you want to save $5000 but don't specify a time frame, it could happen in six months or 20 years from now. Setting a timeframe will keep you focused and motivated to achieve your financial goals.

Pretend you are Usain Bolt running the 100m sprint. Say you want to run it in 9.5 seconds. That means you have to cut 0.08 seconds off of your current personal best. You give yourself three months to achieve this. Firstly, the goal is specific because you need to take 0.08 seconds off of your current time. It is measurable because you measure it in seconds. It is achievable because you have accomplished a similar time in the past. It is realistic because you are the world record holder in the 100m sprints, and finally, it is timely because you have given yourself three months to reach your goal. But remember, you aren't Usain Bolt, so if you were to give yourself the same goal, yes, it would be specific, measurable, and timely, but it would not be realistic or achievable. A goal needs to have all five components for it to be considered a good and reachable goal.

3. How to make your goals work

Setting your financial goals is an excellent strategy, and making them SMART simplifies it even further. However, there are some crucial tips that you should consider to ensure you meet these goals.

Consider inflation

Inflation isn't something many people will consider when creating a goal, but it is a vital consideration since it has an impact on your financial goals. Interest can be very useful for long-term goals like retirement funds or savings because they allow your money to appreciate as time goes on. The value of one dollar was worth significantly more 100 years ago, but now it is significantly less valuable. Interest rates make sure that your money retains its value. Remember to keep inflation and the appreciation/depreciation of your money in mind when making financial goals.

Keep a record

Keeping a record of your goals will keep you motivated and on track. You will be able to see which goals you have completed and which goals you still need to work towards. Remember to update your list of goals as you make progress towards financial stability. You may include information on your progress, how you achieved your goals, and what you can improve on in the future. These records can also provide the motivation your family needs to work towards the next goals. When people can identify areas where they have made progress, it pushes them to work harder. This is what a record will do for your family.

Discuss with a financial advisor

You may not be a financial professional, but there are people out there who give excellent financial advice. These professionals can be an asset to you when making investment decisions. Through your discussion with a financial advisor, you will be able to find out the best investment option for you and your family.

Identify what your family's spending habits are

Creating a budget for your family is easy to do in theory, but certain things make it difficult to put into practice. The spending habits of your family play a role in determining the success of any budget you create. Do your family members have bad spending habits? The problem with bad spending habits in a family is that it affects every individual in the unit. If your household includes four individuals, having a single individual with bad spending habits can get you all into serious financial problems. To help you get past this problem, this first step is to identify any noticeable spending habits that may be negatively affecting your financial situation. There are many of these, and here are some to help you get started:

Instant gratification

As human beings, we all work hard to achieve the goals that matter most to us. Once we achieve these goals, we want some form of reward for our actions. This comes in the form of instant gratification. Instant gratification is about getting fulfillment instantly without wanting any form of delay. This is not only applicable to finances but is perpetuated by the internet and social media. When you post a photo of yourself, you get likes, and people comment on the photos. This kind of instant gratification influences many people as you no longer have to physically go and see someone if you crave attention; you can just post a quick selfie and derive sufficient pleasure from it. The opposite of instant gratification is delayed gratification. To explain this using your finances, think about the salary you earn at the end of the month. If you are left with $5,000 after paying off your monthly expenses, how do you spend it? For an individual who seeks instant gratification, purchasing new clothes or shoes is an excellent way to spend this money. On the other hand, an individual who seeks delayed gratification will choose to invest this money.

This is what makes instant gratification a bad spending habit. It prevents you from seeing ways to make your money work for you. Spending everything you earn on things you don't need will always put you in a tight spot financially. To help you determine if instant gratification is a spending habit your family struggles with, look out for any of the following:

- **Your family does not have an emergency fund.** When you spend everything you earn, it is impossible to set aside any amount of money as savings. Building an emergency fund requires you to plan for the future—a form of delayed gratification. If you have a family and lack an emergency fund, it is a clear indication of poor spending habits.

- **You spend on impulse.** Yes, impulse spending is common among individuals who desire instant gratification. When you see something you want, you're willing to get it without considering the impact it might have on your budget. Sometimes, people can be emotional spenders and tend to buy things when they feel sad or lonely. Keep track of when you are spending and why in order to prevent this.

- **Your credit card debt is high.** Why do you need a credit card? Is it to support your family when cash is temporarily unavailable, or do you have one to support an unhealthy lifestyle? Having a lot of credit card debt can be an indication of poor spending habits because instead of saving and waiting to buy things, you may impulse buy and rack up debt on your card. If your credit card debt is high, this also suggests that you don't have enough money to pay it off. Frequent use of credit cards is another effect of instant gratification. This is because most purchases you make using this card are not accounted for in your budget. A credit card should be used solely for emergencies.

Cars

Purchasing a car is an act that can cause a significant setback in your family's financial situation. Buying a car is not necessarily a bad idea if you do it right. However, there are several mistakes people often make when buying a new vehicle. Some of these include:

- Choosing to buy a new car
- Overlooking other costs of purchase
- Not making a down payment; and
- Only considering monthly payments.

One thing many individuals and families fail to understand is that buying a new car is not a great investment for the family. Regardless of how enticing the deal may seem, you will end up on the losing end in the long run. In addition to the high costs you incur, cars also depreciate rapidly. This means you will lose a lot of money if you decide to trade-in the vehicle too soon. This is an issue your family will have to deal with if car purchases are too frequent.

You must find a way to ensure you save as much money as you can on your car expenses. There are several steps you can take to do this, and one of the most important is to purchase a car with cash. One of the benefits of purchasing with cash is that it limits how much you can spend. Using this method when you need to purchase your car will ensure you don't get enticed by a newer model that costs a lot more than you can afford. To purchase a car with cash, you will need to save for it. What option makes more sense to you: saving for a car that costs $20,000 or saving for a car that costs $4,000? Saving for a car that costs $4,000 is the better option financially, but many people don't look at things from this perspective. In reality, most new model vehicles will cost you upwards of $15,000, which may increase depending on the agreement you have with a dealer.

The average individual will not notice this high cost since they focus solely on the monthly payment—which can be as low as $500 per month. When a dealer gives you the option to pay $500 per month over four years, you end up paying more for the vehicle. Considering the smaller amount you pay monthly, you may not feel the impact immediately. However, when you complete the payment in four years, the car will have depreciated in value. If you decide to sell it at this point, getting someone to pay $15,000 for the vehicle may be impossible.

A better option is to save up and buy a used car. Although this option comes with a few issues, there are several benefits to buying a secondhand car. First, you spend less on purchasing the car. You can get a great used vehicle for $8,000-$10,000. Another benefit of buying a used vehicle in cash is that you don't risk losing the car if you default on a car loan payment. This is a problem that can occur if you lose your job during the repayment period and have purchased a new car. Used cars also have a lower insurance cost when compared to new vehicles. However, you must also consider that they have more significant wear-and-tear than a new vehicle.

Dining Out

Buying your next meal from a restaurant is always appealing—especially after working long hours. This is an option many families tend to choose over cooking meals at home because it is quicker and easier. However, eating out can hinder the financial growth of your family. When purchasing food or eating at a restaurant, other things can increase your bill. You have to spend money on tips, drinks, and the cost of getting to the restaurant. Eating out too often is another way many families spend above their means. As you get further into the month, most of the eating out expenses begin to reflect on your credit card.

An easy way to overcome this habit is to start preparing your meals as a family. You could start by learning to prepare the things you order the most. For some families, this may be pizza. If you discover most of your food expenses come from ordering pizza, then you can go online to find various homemade pizza recipes to try out. When you try out these recipes, you will discover that you can get fresh pizza at a much lower price than a delivery.

Another step you must take is to create a meal plan. Most families eat out because they don't make meal plans at home. Without a plan, you may not have the necessary ingredients you need for a meal. When you make a meal plan, you can plan ahead and go to the grocery shop to purchase all the ingredients you need. To help you save on groceries, you can create a meal plan based on items that are on sale at your local grocer. If you know time is a limiting factor for you, you should try preparing meals for the week and storing them. This means you won't have to prepare meals every day, and it saves you a lot of time in the process.

The final step to take is to stock your pantry. This is something you must frequently do to ensure you don't eat out. There are so many things you can store in your pantry to make a quick meal when you need to. You can store cans of soup, a box of pancake mix, spices, canned food, and many more items in the pantry for your next meal. Plan ahead and make sure you have everything to make a delicious meal at home. Keep track of the purchases you make and compare your budgets. Did you actually save more when you cooked at home as opposed to when you dined out regularly?

Vacations

Having a clear definition of the needs and wants of your family can help you cut down on certain expenses. To be honest, vacations are often what your family needs. Work can be overwhelming, and sometimes you just want to get away from reality for a few days or weeks. There are several benefits to going on vacation, including:

- **Promotes family bonding.** Spending time together as a family can be difficult when you consider how busy you all are. Parents have to go to work, and kids have to study or engage in extracurricular activities. With the impact of technology, the little free time many individuals have is often spent on social media or watching TV programs. By taking a vacation with the family, you create an opportunity for everyone to bond and connect.

- **Provides valuable experiences.** The experiences your household will get from a vacation can't be replaced with the items you purchase. This is what makes vacations irreplaceable in most cases. Unlike the toys, games, and smartphones, the memories you create on vacation will last a lifetime. If you must take your family on vacation for this reason, then you must find ways to reduce your expenses by limiting your purchase of the latest gadgets or toys.

- **It helps develop social awareness in children.** Taking your children on vacation is one way to improve their social awareness. Vacations allow them to interact with people outside their community, city, region, or country. This means they get to learn things from new cultural perspectives. Although they learn some of these things in school, they will do this on a practical level when on vacation.

Despite vacations being categorized as expensive and time-consuming, they may be a crucial part of creating the right family atmosphere for financial stability. I'm not saying you should go to the most expensive hotels and order room service while charging it all to your credit card. There are many deals and discounts available for families who want to go on holiday. Stay at a budget conscious hotel and eat local food. You also don't have to go on vacation every three months. If you plan it right, you can go once every year or every two years. However, if vacationing is not part of your family or financial value plan and you would rather spend money on something else, then you can tailor your actions to your desires.

4. What Are Your Family's Non-Negotiable Expenses?

Every family has its own non-negotiables. These are expenses they must incur every month. Changing these expenses is going to take a lot of time and can be very difficult. For most families, these non-negotiables include food, clothes, and shelter. However, some additional expenses fit into this category. Perhaps you or one of your family members has a chronic illness and requires regular medication. This is considered a non-negotiable. However, sometimes non-negotiables can be reevaluated. While food, clothes, and housing are non-negotiable, you don't need to eat out, buy designer clothes, and live in a mansion. In this way, you can readjust your spending to live within your means and still cater to the non-negotiable needs of your family. To encourage your family to change their spending on non-negotiables, there are specific actions you need to take. The most crucial step is to break down the non-negotiable expenses into sub-categories. Here is a break-down of some of the common non-negotiable expenses:

Housing

What your family spends on housing should be easy to identify, but are you capturing the accurate figures? Although expenses such as mortgage and rent may be fixed for a period, others such as insurance and property taxes may fluctuate. Here is a list of some of the extra housing costs you may incur:

- Mortgage payment
- Mortgage insurance
- Rent

- Property taxes
- Owner's or renter's insurance
- Maintenance fees/costs

When you carefully assess each of these sub-categories, it becomes easier to identify where and when there is an increase in your housing expenses.

Food

This is another non-negotiable expense that you need to analyze. Every family needs to eat, so it isn't something that can be eliminated. When analyzing your food expenses, you need to separate dining out costs from grocery expenses. This is because the food expenses are non-negotiable, while the dining out expenses are negotiable.

Medical Expenses

Budgeting for a non-negotiable expense like medical expenses can be tricky. This is because these expenses are usually unplanned. Therefore, it is possible to overspend on this expense sometimes and underspend at other times. Coming up with a rough estimate of how much you spend on monthly medical expenses is one way to start. You can also choose to find the average of your past costs to determine this value. For families with individuals who suffer from chronic illnesses, this task won't be as straightforward because the expenses will likely be far higher and more regular than those of the average family. Some of the additional expenses you can expect to pay include the following:

- Doctors' visits (or paramedical visits)
- Health insurance

- Prescribed medications
- Surgery
- Overnight stay
- Emergency visits

When estimating the medical non-negotiables, it is a good idea to budget higher than you spend monthly. This will give you some room for emergencies if they do come up. If they don't, you can channel this additional cash to the medical expenses for the next month or add it to your savings.

5. Recommendations for Spending

Even though some expenses are important, it is still possible to cut down on them. Here, we will be looking into the best practice regarding how much money families *should* be spending in each major expense category of the family budget. What should you be doing? It's simple. As a family trying to create a budget, one area where you will have significant issues is allocating funds to each budget category. You can use different methods when allocating funds, but this section will take you through the most popular method—mainly, the 50/30/20 method.

The 50/30/20 Method

This is one of the most popular budget allocation methods. It is also the simplest method for families that are new to the idea of budgeting. It suggests that 50% of your funds should go to the family needs, 30% to the wants, and 20% to various savings accounts.

- **Needs (50%)**

For this method to work, the family must have a clear description of their needs and wants. The needs are the expenses or bills that are non-negotiable, as discussed in the previous section. They are essential for the survival of the family. Expenses that fall into this category include the following:

- Health care
- Utilities
- Mortgage payments/rent
- Minimum debt repayment
- Groceries
- Car loan payments
- Insurance

These are the things that you must have, and not the things that you want. This category should take up 50% of your monthly income after-tax. For families whose needs exceed 50% of their monthly income, you may have to find ways to cut down on some costs. This may involve moving into a smaller house, making a lifestyle change, using public transportation, or choosing a cheaper insurance package. Carefully assess your spending to find what works for the family.

- **Wants (30%)**

Your wants are the expenses you incur that are not essential to your survival. For anyone seeking to build wealth and gain financial freedom, this is one area where you can trim down on expenses. Some of the costs in this category include vacations, eating out, new gadgets, new clothes, etc. There are several ways to cut down on expenses in this category. You can start by cooking at home to avoid eating out, working out at home instead of getting a gym membership, and buying clothes only when you need to instead of spending money on new items based on a new fashion season.

Some expensive lifestyle choices you make also fall into this category. For example, deciding to buy a designer bag and not an unbranded bag is a want. Paying for multiple cable TV packages when you can subscribe to a lower cost streaming service is also a want. Identifying these wants is necessary to help you reduce your expenses. Regardless of what you list under this category, you shouldn't be spending more than 30% of your income. Although these are expenses that make life enjoyable and entertaining for the family, be sure to find ways to enjoy life without having to spend all of your money.

- **Savings (20%)**

Compared to the other two components of this method, saving requires the least amount of money, but don't be fooled because this amount will build up over time. Contributing 20% of your income to savings will allow you to build a comfortable nest egg that you can use for emergency funds and investment purposes. An appropriate emergency fund has a balance of at least six months of the family's living expenses. Other areas where your savings may go to include retirement account contributions, stock market investments, or mutual fund accounts.

When considering the savings category, you can also allocate some of the money to debt repayment. This differs from the needs that have a minimum debt repayment. Once you pay off all your debt, you will have more cash to build up your savings faster. You must divert all leftover money from the wants and needs category into your savings at the end of the budget period.

6. Other Helpful Methods

The 50/30/20 method is useful, but it doesn't give a breakdown of your budget. For some individuals, having a breakdown of each expense is crucial for the success of the budget. As a family, this helps since your costs will differ from that of other families. To use any other budgeting method effectively, the first step is to make a list of all your expenses. These expenses can include some or all of the following:

- Child care
- Transportation
- Taxes
- Food
- Housing
- Clothing
- Savings
- Debt repayment
- Medical expenses
- Utilities
- Insurance
- Entertainment and recreation

- Personal spending

From this list, you can then separate the expenses into the negotiables and non-negotiables. To get you on the right track, here is a breakdown of how much you should be spending on each category:

- **Housing:** Your housing expenses include your mortgage payments, rent, maintenance costs, and property taxes. This is often the most considerable expense on your budget, so you can allocate 25-35% of your income towards housing expenses.

- **Food:** This is a non-negotiable expense. Since you are trying to manage your finances effectively, don't include dining out expenses in this category. If you use this method, 10-15% of the family income is enough to cover food expenses.

- **Transportation:** You need to move from your home to the grocery store or your workplace. Other members of your family will also need to go to important places, like school. Therefore, there is no way to eliminate the cost of transportation from your budget. You can budget 10-15% of the family income for transportation to cover your gas, parking, tolls, and other fees.

- **Healthcare and medical:** Healthcare is a non-negotiable expense and should make up about 10% of your income.

- **Savings, debt payments, investing:** Like with the 50/30/20 method, you should set aside 20% of your income. This is a vital category in your budget. The impact may not be noticeable immediately, but in the future, your efforts will yield rewards.

- **Utilities:** To live comfortably in the home, you need to pay for electricity, or gas, internet, and water. These utilities are also non-negotiable. With 10% of the family income, you should have a home with well-functioning utilities.

With this breakdown, you can complete your budget with whatever you have left. Remember to identify what works for your family as it will differ from household to household.

Using Technology to Help You Budget

Technology can be extremely useful to you if used appropriately. You can travel, communicate, prepare meals, learn, and do so much more with technology at your side. Technology also offers excellent benefits to the way you handle your budget. Depending on how you utilize technology, you can cut down on how much you spend monthly and boost your savings in the process. Some of the ways through which technology can help with budgeting are:

Price Comparisons

An excellent budget is one that contains all of your essential expenses at a reasonable price. To get the most beneficial prices of various items, you need to have a way to compare prices from different stores. With access to the internet, this is possible. There are various tools or apps that help you find out the best places to buy certain items. These include information on deals, sales, and other promotional information. Some of the products you can compare include insurance, groceries, gasoline, and consumer goods. Since these are some of the essential items in your budget, finding ways to reduce how much you spend on them will help you reach and maintain your budgeting goals.

Monitor Your Finances Anytime and Anywhere

For a successful family budget, you need to have the opportunity to manage your finances from anywhere in the world. With technology, this is possible. You have the option to manage both your expenses and savings whenever you want. Using your bank app, you can track your expenses and income for the month from the comfort of your home. There are apps that allow you to transfer funds, receive funds, invest, and check your balances from anywhere in the world.

Automate Processes

There are periods when your work can become overwhelming. When this happens, it can be easy to forget some crucial things you need to do. As a result, you may fail to pay essential bills and end up incurring late fees. By utilizing technology, you can automate the regular payments you need to make. Your credit card payments, utility bills, and mortgage payments are some of the payments you can automate. Many bank apps also offer users the option of automating their savings. This feature allows the bank to deduct a specific amount of your income and transfer it into a separate savings account. When you set up this process, you pay yourself first before dealing with your expenses.

Clear Clutter

If you decide to maintain your finances on paper, this can create paper clutter in the home. It also becomes difficult to find vital information when you need it the most. On the other hand, using digital means to maintain your finances simplifies the process and minimizes paper clutter.

Best Budgeting Software

Budgeting software is any program or application that helps simplify the budgeting process. Such apps will offer options to manage, create, and monitor a budget to simplify the process. Most of these apps provide users with the option to sync their financial accounts. When you do this, the app can automatically download the necessary information it needs to give you a clear picture of your financial position. Since there are various budgeting apps available, there will be differences in the methods available for budgeting on each platform.

Like with many apps available online, there are free and paid versions of budgeting software. Some free options offer excellent services, but these may not match what you get with the paid versions. For the paid versions, the subscription price can range from $3 to $15 a month. Some apps offer only a yearly subscription to users, and these subscriptions are often cheaper than the monthly payments. In this section, you will learn about some of the most popular budgeting software/apps available.

1. EveryDollar

The EveryDollar app is available to users on Android, iOS, and desktop platforms. You can do many things on this app, and these functions help simplify the budgeting process for your family:

- **Set up monthly budgets:** Like every other budgeting app, you can find on the market, this app offers users the option to create a budget. This option is a monthly budget that you can create if you take these steps:

- Input the income of the family: Create a list of the family expenses from the essentials (needs) to the non-essentials (wants).

- Create a zero-based budget: This is a budgeting option in which you input all your income and then subtract all of your expenses to get a zero value. Through this budgeting method, you can account for every penny you spend and the effect it has on your financial situation.

- **Monitor your spending:** Tracking your spending is a crucial step in controlling your expenses. The EveryDollar app gives you the option of including your expenses whenever you need to. This can be at home or in your car after completing a purchase. If this manual process is stressful, then you can sync the app to your bank account. This allows the transactions you make to appear automatically in the budget. Now, you can place each transaction in the appropriate budget category. The availability of the app on mobile devices makes it easy for users to check-in whenever they want. It doesn't matter if you're at home or work; you can choose to check your budget on your smartphone or desktop anytime. This option to check your budget frequently is an easy way for individuals to swiftly address any issue of overspending before it leads to debt.

- **Include a due date on bills:** It is easy to forget about the bills you need to pay when you are preoccupied with other things. With the EveryDollar app, you can ensure you always pay your bills on time. This is possible through the option of adding a due date to your bills. As long as you take the time to go on the app frequently, you will always get a reminder.

- **Set up target funds:** The option to set up a savings goal is an excellent feature for anyone looking to make a significant purchase. You can also use it in preparation for expenses that you incur once a year. Seeing your progress usually provides the motivation you need to work harder.

2. You Need a Budget

If you are a novice in creating and using budgets, the You Need a Budget platform is an excellent option for you. Some of the features it offers include a customization feature, color-coding of financial goals, and swift transaction importation. It was launched in September 2004 and has quickly become a favorite among individuals seeking healthy financial growth. The various categories on the app help you account for every saving or spending activity you engage in. The easy access to the zero-sum budgeting method enables you to pay off your debt quickly.

With the excellent service you get from the app, it is understandable that you won't be able to get it for free. However, there is a 34-day free trial. This is over a month, so it is enough time for you to determine if this app is the best option for you and your family or not. You can download the app on your Android, iOS, or Alexa devices. The paid plan starts at US$11.99 a month, or you can get a discount price of US$84 for a year. The app is very effective since the model requires you to import your various financial accounts. This helps in providing a visual representation of funds allocation and spending activities. The report you get from the app gives you a breakdown of your progress towards the long-term financial goals you have set up for your family.

You should note that this app doesn't have the bill payment option. Actions such as tax planning, retirement, and investing are also excluded from the financial information available on this app. Pros for this app include the ability to discover the consequences of spending habits through the questions and color-coding on the app. The app is also user-friendly and has instructions for new users to follow and better understand how it works. Cons for this app include the fact that the service is expensive in comparison to other available options.

3. Mint

This is another great application that will help you with your budget. The dashboard provides an overview of your financial status—this includes information on your credit score, funds, bills, debt, assets, and retirement. It is a free app available to users on Android, iOS, and online platforms. Intuit is the company behind Mint, and they have other popular products such as TurboTax and QuickBooks. As of Fall 2020, on both the Apple Store and Google Play Store, Mint has a rating of above 4.4 stars.

When using the Mint platform, it assesses your financial behavior and then provides suggestions that match this behavior. It also uses this financial behavior to help you create the most effective budget for your family. If you get into a situation where your funds are getting low or your bills are due for payment, you will receive an app alert. However, a bill payment function is not available on the app. You can sync your financial accounts to the app, but it is common for users to encounter issues with the app's syncing feature.

Pros for this app include that the app allows users to view their credit score for free. Based on your spending habits, the app can also generate a budget automatically. Cons include reports that syncing transactions to personal Mint accounts have been known to present technical issues on occasion. You have to export reports from a CSV file to view them, and it is not possible to customize budget categories.

4. Clarity Money

If you know anything about the banking industry, then the name Goldman Sachs shouldn't be new to you. These banking giants own the Clarity Money tool. This is a free tool that is available on both the iOS and Android platforms. With this app, users can monitor and cancel third-party subscriptions that they rarely use. You can also link your accounts to the app, organize your expenses, and track your spending on the app. Although you can create a spending plan on the app, the plan is limited to a week. You can automate savings on Clarity Money, but there is no option to customize the app categories. The dashboard gives users information about their credit usage, spending summaries, some suggested products, and more. The app offers to help you manage your money effectively.

Pros for this app are that it is easy to use, you can find and eliminate unnecessary subscriptions, and the product recommendations included are helpful in finding areas to reduce your expenses. Cons include that you can only create weekly budgets, the categories are not customizable, and you can only reach customer support via email.

5. PocketGuard

This is an excellent app for families who need to reduce their debt rapidly. You can use it to track excess money in your budget and create spending limits for you and the family. PocketGuard has been in operation since 2015 but isn't as popular as many of the other apps on this list. There is a free version of the app, but the paid version is where it truly shines. You gain access to features such as cash purchases tracking, transaction data export, customization of budget categories, and unlimited goal creation. You can get the app on both Android, iOS, and the internet. When using the app, it gives you updates on how much you have to spend, which is useful in maintaining your budget.

Pros for this app include the fact that it uses your financial goals to create a budget, it indicates the free money you have after allocating funds to your savings and bills, and there is a free version available if you don't want to commit to the paid version. Cons include the presence of ads and email solicitations, limited functionality in the free version, and a lack of functionality in the web version.

So, now you know how to set up a budget for you and your family and why it is important. Budgets are a great way to make your goals happen. If you are not technologically inclined, get creative with your budgets! However, there are so many helpful programs and apps out there that can help you keep track of your money while you are working and side-hustling your way to early retirement. Don't be afraid to consult a financial advisor if you are having a tough time allocating your funds or if you have a particularly unique family situation.

Chapter 4

How to Eliminate Debt and Why it's so Important to do so

"A debt problem is, at its core, a budgeting problem."

—Natalie Pace

Debt is the money you owe. You could be indebted to a friend, a business, the bank, and much more public and private entities. The concept of debt is quite simple. If you have three apples for an apple pie and you need four, you might find yourself knocking on the neighbor's door asking for an apple. Now, this apple comes at a price, and nothing in this life is free. You don't have enough apples to make the pie or pay your neighbor back, so you take the apple and promise to pay them back at a later date. Money works the same way, except being several thousand dollars in debt is far more problematic than owing someone an apple. For debt to happen, there must be a lender and a borrower—an entity that has the resources versus an entity that does not. This transaction does not end here, however, as the debt must be paid back, and until the borrower has enough money, this is not possible.

The opposite of debt is credit, and the two concepts are intertwined. It's kind of like a see-saw. When one is high, the other is low. Credit is what the lender has instead of debt. Interestingly, the Latin root of the word *credit* means *he believes*. This implies a sense of trust in the relationship between lender and borrower. In other words, whoever is giving credit does so with the belief that the debtor will honor the promise to pay the credit. Both credit and debt are all about deferred payments. The only major difference is that credit is an asset, while debt is a liability. While the creditor anticipates gains, the debtor anticipates losing money.

Do You Have to Borrow to Incur Debt?

At first, the answer might seem obvious, but the truth of the matter might shock you. Ultimately, you don't have to borrow money to incur debt. There are several ways to incur debt without borrowing. Hiring a long-term service will mean that the service is completed before you make the payment. Essentially, you are indebted to the person who has provided the service until you pay them. You didn't borrow any money or take out a loan, but there was still a transaction that occurred. Perhaps something more unexpected happens, like you get into a minor car accident and hit the side of a building. You have to pay for the damages and are now effectively indebted to the owner of the building. Again, you didn't borrow any money or take out a loan, but you caused damage to property and are now liable to pay for the repairs. You could also be indebted to the government in the form of taxes. Think of all the estate taxes. Those are debts you owe the government even though you definitely didn't borrow a penny from them. There are many ways you can incur debt without borrowing from any person or organization. However, when you're in debt, how you got into debt may not really matter; the key is to find a way out.

Why It's Important to Get Rid of Your Debt

Getting into debt is easy but finding your way out of it is the harder part. Sometimes, it can be incredibly difficult to gather the motivation and resources to pay off debt. For many people, it becomes a part of life. They accept it as something they have to put up with, and instead of pushing against it, they start to feel comfortable in their debt. The problem is, debt is not only your problem; it becomes your entire family's problem. It makes taking care of your children and setting them up for the future really difficult. Also, if you have a bad credit score, it will affect your ability to buy a house or car in the future. This could be a major setback in the long-run as you may want to invest in assets later in life.

However, with discipline, patience, and dedication, paying off even a very significant amount of debt is possible. Paying off debt doesn't only relieve you of pressure from creditors; it helps to enhance your financial health. Instead of using your money to pay debts, you can use it to invest and build wealth for the future. If you have ever been on the fence about paying off your debt or just falling deeper into the debt-hole, here are some reasons why you should consider paying off your debt first.

Financial Benefits of Paying Off Debt

- **It frees up your finances for investments.**

Investments not only provide an alternative source of income; they also serve as a means to secure your future financially. Unfortunately, being in debt has a way of discouraging investments. This is why you should endeavor to pay off all your debt, to free up your finances for investment opportunities.

Though some people try to invest while knee-deep in debt, such a decision could be counterproductive in the long-run. For instance, if you owe a $10,000 debt that incurs a $100 interest each month, you will be indebted by an additional $1,200 at the end of 12 months. This means you will have to pay off $11,200 in debt if you choose to invest rather than pay off the debt. On the other hand, you can choose to spend a chunk of your cash on repaying your debt in, say, two months and begin investing when your debt has been paid. At the end of the two-month period, you will only have to pay $10,200, rather than an additional $1,000.

- **It frees up your income for other expenses.**

Apart from giving you the opportunity to invest, paying off your debt will also free up your income for other expenses. If you are constantly in debt, the amount you use in servicing that debt will eat up a chunk of your income. For example, if you are servicing a $200,000 30-year mortgage, which comes at 4.5% interest, payments on that particular mortgage alone will eat $1,013 of what you earn every month.

What's worse is that almost 50% of the monthly payment could go towards offsetting the interest rather than actually building equity on the house. If you pay off your debt faster, then that $1,013 will be available to you in any capacity you desire. You could put it into a savings account or simply alleviate some of the pressure around your monthly expenses. On the other hand, if you defer paying off your debt, in just ten years of servicing your mortgage, you would have spent around $121,560 on mortgage debt alone. I'm sure you can think of a few things you would much rather pay for.

- **It frees up money for early retirement.**

It's the dream, isn't it? Work until you are 55 and retire on a sandy beach somewhere to sip margaritas and listen to the ocean for the rest of your life. One of the things holding you back from actualizing this fantasy could be your debt. That is why paying it off and making it your first financial priority will help set you up for the future. You don't want to be paying off bank loans on the sunny coast of Costa Rica.

You might find it incredibly hard to save for retirement with debtors constantly breathing down your neck. Whether it is your mortgage, credit card, or any debt you're holding that consumes chunks of money, it would better be suited for your retirement savings. It might be unrealistic to retire if you have to put your kids through college or pay for school fees. That's why paying your debt off and investing is a more effective route to early retirement.

- **It lessens financial risk.**

One of the most devastating effects of being in debt is the huge financial risk it places you in. Whenever you are in huge debt, you are practically one financial problem away from disaster. If you don't have emergency savings to fall back on, the outcome could be devastating. A health problem, job loss, or being financially incapacitated in any way could be far more debilitating if you are already struggling with debt.

You might be wondering what would happen if you just let your debt be and did nothing about it. Surely you could live on credit until you no longer need to? Well, not quite. Leaving debt unsettled could lead to some very serious repercussions and legal action. Essentially, you could:

- Be sued for not paying your debt

- Have your car repossessed in the case of a car loan

- Lose your home because of foreclosure or be evicted for not paying rent, or

- Have to file for bankruptcy.

Being free of debt means that you don't even have to think about these risks and possibilities. Living debt-free gives your budget space, so you don't have to constantly stay wary of an unfortunate event that might be financially detrimental and take away from your family's future.

- **It helps to improve your credit score.**

Your credit rating can be affected by debt. If you have many loans and credit cards that are close to the limit, you will have a lower score. Having a bad credit score can run you up to thousands of dollars in higher interest rates yearly. Higher interest rates make it a lot harder for you to pay off your debt, keeping you in the debt trap. Your credit score begins to improve as you start paying off your debt. Having a good credit score will set you up with a few benefits:

- Finding apartments will be more comfortable as landlords check credit scores to know if you will be a reliable tenant

- Your insurance company will offer lower premiums

- Securing future loans with better interest rates will be a lot easier

- You get better cell phone service deals

- Employers check credit scores to know if you are a reliable employee. A good credit score can give you a better chance of getting your dream job.

- **It can make you eligible for better job opportunities.**

Believe it or not, the weight of debt can slow you down at work as well. You might find it difficult to sleep as thoughts of money keep you up at night. This stress, in turn, affects your productivity at your work. It is even worse if you have to deal with debt collectors at work. They impair your productivity and interrupt your workflow by calling in at the office. Debt collectors can even make things worse and more embarrassing by directly contacting your employer in a bid to locate you. Such a situation can strain communication between you and your managers. Paying off your debt means that you will have a lot more motivation to work harder when you know that you get to keep any money you make instead of paying off debt.

Additionally, paying off your debt could allow you to find a better job because you won't be held down by pressure and necessity anymore. You will be in a financially comfortable position and will be able to make decisions for your happiness and not only your survival. If you have remained at a job you hate because you need to raise funds to offset your credit card bills or other forms of debt, you will have the freedom to search for a new and more rewarding job the moment you have paid off your debt.

The Relationship Benefits of Paying Off Debt

Apart from the direct financial benefits that being debt-free can bring to your life, a debt-free life can significantly enhance your relationships with others. Financial pressure can create a lot of tension and anxiety in the family unit and among friends.

Wouldn't it be nice to go out and have dinner with your family or get your child the toy they want instead of sitting at home worrying about money? Living a debt-free life won't only improve your career and general wellbeing; it will also help your relationships.

- **It strengthens relationships.**

Depression, anger, and fear are just some of the negative emotions that debt can stir up. While these feelings are usually within you, they sometimes spill over into your interactions and relationships with your friends, family, or work colleagues. Stress manifests in a multitude of ways, and if you are not careful, you could end up pushing your family and friends away instead of asking them for help and support. A life without debt means that you don't have a burden hanging over your head. You can laugh and enjoy time with the people whom you love without having to worry about how you could have been working an extra shift at work instead. You won't have to second guess all of your decisions, and you will be able to go on vacations and treat your family. There are enough stressors in this world without having debt, so lighten your load and live a debt-free life.

- **It leads to a better marriage.**

Money problems and debt are some of the most common causes of marital problems. How can you be comfortable and happy when you and your partner or spouse are constantly worried about money? What if the balance in income is skewed to one side? How do you logically and effectively handle this dynamic in a marriage? Even if spouses see debt as a common problem, the stress that exists because of that debt can be quite problematic. This stress is part of what causes friction among spouses who are dealing with huge debt. Sometimes, couples blame each other for incurring debt, and this can lead to mistrust, loss of confidence in each other, and a general deterioration in relationships. There have been situations where partners have opted to part ways because of financial instability. Therefore, it is important to work together when handling debt. However, it is even better not to have debt at all.

- **It promotes better parenting around finances.**

As a parent, you have an enormous financial responsibility towards your children. A great way to help you honor these responsibilities is by clearing off your debt. When you pay off your debt, you free up your income, which means you can have extra money to invest in your children's wellbeing and future. This is the beginning of building generational wealth for your family. This could be in the form of education or saving up some cash that they can use when they are older and more independent. Also, when you live a debt-free life, you tend to be less tense or stressed and will, therefore, have a better relationship with your children.

- **It helps others.**

If you are struggling with your own financial issues, helping others is probably the last thing you are capable of doing. However, living a debt-free life will give you the ability to help the people around you. Whether that help comes in monetary, emotional, or physical form, you will have the capacity to support and aid someone else through their troubles. Plus, if you have been struggling with debt for a long time, helping someone might make you feel better and more confident about yourself. You will be able to see how far you have come and thank yourself for working so hard. Reap the benefits of your dedication and sow seeds of financial stability for the future.

The Mental Benefits of Paying Off Debt

- **It reduces stress.**

Owing money can be extremely stressful. The uncertainty and insecurity surrounding your future might become unbearable and lead to symptoms of depression and anxiety. All the decisions you make when you don't live a debt-free life feel like they could either make or break you. Suddenly, treating yourself to a quick coffee becomes a much bigger decision than it needs to be. You feel immense guilt when you spend any money on even the smallest pleasures, and the pressure of having to work to pay off what you owe weighs you down. Living debt-free means that you don't have to worry about those things anymore, and your financial stress will be relieved.

- **It improves mental health.**

Debt causes more than just stress. Scientists can trace several mental problems that can be caused by being in debt. According to a Northwestern study, people in a lot of debt were about 13% more likely to experience symptoms of depression than the average person. In 2014, a study was published documenting similar results in adults over 50. The higher the debt, the more severe the symptoms experienced were. In extreme cases, people who have large amounts of debt might resort to committing suicide in an effort to escape their financial restraints and lighten the load on their families. Studies have reported that people who have overwhelming amounts of debt from student loans can exhibit suicidal tendencies—being debt-free releases you from the clutches of depression or anxiety caused by financial pressures and constraints. Having no debt is almost as significant as having a high income in terms of the effect it has on overall levels of happiness.

- **It promotes self-esteem.**

Your self-esteem can be negatively impacted by debt. According to psychologists, people who are in debt try to create the illusion that their lives are perfect. They try to hide their situation from their friends and family by buying fancy clothes or driving fast cars when, in reality, the situation is completely opposite. Trying to keep up appearances will only leave you in further debt and feeling inadequate. Focus on things that make you happy and that don't require money. It might be difficult, and you may feel like a failure some days. It is important to recognize that you are not a failure; you just need to make different financial decisions for yourself and your family. On the flip side, paying off your debt is just the boost your self-confidence craves. It is a big deal to live a debt-free life, and if you can accomplish that, then you have a lot to be proud of.

- **It improves cognitive function.**

Debt is more than just an emotional problem. It can also affect your ability to reason and think logically. In 2017, Frontiers in Psychology published a study highlighting some of the cognitive issues caused by a deteriorating financial situation. These included self-control problems, impaired attention spans, and weak working memory. The problem is, when you are in a stressful situation, you need your brain to be sharp and in control. However, because your cognitive function may be weak due to the effects of debt, your decision-making skills are impaired and can therefore add to your financial problems instead of clear them up. Debt also makes you less skilled at identifying and evaluating risks, causing you to take risks that could result in long-term losses. Paying off your debt, fortunately, addresses these cognitive problems. In 2017, families with high levels of debt were given large sums of money to pay off these debts. Experts noticed a significant improvement in the participants' cognitive function. Mainly, the participants experienced a reduced level of anxiety and were able to make better decisions.

The Physical Benefits of Paying Off debt

- **It reduces illnesses.**

The stress of having debt can damage not only your finances, your mind, and your relationships; it can also have physical effects on your body. Studies have shown that people who have high levels of debt are generally unhealthier. Debt can be damaging to your health in many ways. In 2008, a study showed that people who experience stress as a result of their financial situation are three times more likely to experience digestive problems than people who have lower levels of debt. They are also twice as susceptible to heart attacks and arrhythmias.

Your immune system can also suffer from chronic stress, placing you at risk of contracting infectious illnesses such as the common cold and flu. Insomnia is another terrible effect of stress caused by worrying about money. When your body is not getting enough rest, it affects your ability to ward off illnesses. Paying your debt gives you both mental and physical relief. The constant stomachaches and headaches that accompany constant overthinking will gradually cease, and you can get back to living a healthy and debt-free life.

- **It normalizes blood pressure.**

High levels of debt can cause your blood pressure to skyrocket. A study by Northwestern indicated that people who had high debt levels had a 1.3% increase in their diastolic blood pressure compared to the average person. The percentage might seem small, but it is more than enough to affect your health negatively. If your blood pressure increases by as little as two points, you are already 15% more likely to suffer from a stroke and 17% more likely to suffer from hypertension. Not only will paying your debt make you feel better, but it could also save your life.

- **It reduces physical pain.**

Studies have suggested that debt can be the cause of some physical pain. In 2008, an AP survey discovered that about 44% of people who experienced debt also suffered from migraines. Experts compared this data to debt-free people, and only 15% of participants suffered from migraines. People with financial stress are also more susceptible to muscle tension and back pain. As you begin to pay off your debts, you will begin to feel less stressed and notice the physical effects of this stress begin to dissipate. Remember to listen to your body. When you are feeling stressed, slow down and take a breath. The debt may feel like you are suffocating, but there is a way out, and you will be okay. Just take it one step at a time.

- **It allows you to take care of your health.**

Aside from the stress that comes with being in debt, owing money can stop you from visiting the doctor. In 2013, the Journal of Health and Social Behavior conducted a study and found that people with a lot of medical debt or credit card debt did not visit the doctor as often as they should. People who are in debt tend to skip dentist and doctor appointments due to the financial burden of these appointments. This is because these appointments cost money, and you will most likely have to spend money on medicine and other medical expenses. Alternatively, people who were debt-free or had low levels of debt were more likely to visit their doctors regularly and stay on top of their health. Paying off your debt will allow you to prioritize your health and visit your doctor or dentist more regularly.

Credit Cards Are Convenient but Be Cautious

Credit cards are a convenient way to pay for things that you don't actually have the money to pay for. While this is the great part about credit cards, it is also one of the riskier aspects of using a credit card. Using a credit card is one of the easiest ways to rack up debt. It's easy to get carried away when you basically have access to money in advance. As you walk into those sparkly shops and the newness hypnotizes you, you walk through the furniture isles and charge a velvet couch and an oak table to your card. You stroll into the designer shops and buy yourself a leather jacket. Before you know it, your card is maxed out, and none of the stores you went to have return policies. See, credit cards can be very useful when you know you can pay them off at the end of the month. However, using money that you don't actually have is extremely risky.

What is a credit card? A credit card is a means of borrowing money and making payments for goods and services. The catch is that when you borrow the money on a credit card, you have to pay it back with interest. Making payments with borrowed money usually involves certain charges and interests that need to be fully paid overtime or on a fixed date. Line of credit is also issued to cardholders to help them borrow money in the form of cash through ATMs, tellers, or credit card convenience checks. The borrowing limits are carefully pre-set by the issuer (the bank) based on the credit rating of the individual. Today, most businesses widely accept credit cards, making it the most common method of transaction. As you spend money on your credit card, you are obligated to pay the money back. If you do so on time and fully, the bank will give you a good credit score.

Understanding Credit Cards

When compared with other forms of consumer loans, credit cards charge a higher annual interest rate for borrowing. The amount of interest is usually added to the credit card debt a month after purchase. So, in order to avoid high-interest rates and paying more than you borrowed, your credit card payments should be on time. There is no grace period given for new charges if you still owe money from previous charges. Before interest is demanded upon any purchase, the bank must give a 21-day grace period. That is why it is good to pay off balances before the expiration of the grace period. Daily interests amount to higher interest charges when the balance is not paid compared to monthly interest rates. However, these regulations and structures vary from bank to bank and country to country. Make sure you check with your credit card provider on what is expected of you and which rules you should be following. Also, make sure that you choose a bank that offers reasonable interest rates; otherwise, you risk losing out on your money for no reason.

Types of Credit Cards

The most popular types of credit cards are Mastercard, Visa, American Express, and Discover. They are issued by credit unions, banks, and other financial institutions. To attract customers, many credit card companies give incentives such as gift certificates, hotel room rentals, airline miles, and other attractive benefits. They also give cash back on purchases. These are known as rewards.

Branded versions of these credit cards are often issued with the store's name imprinted on the card to ensure customer loyalty. It is easier to obtain a store credit card than a standard credit card from a bank. This is because store credit cards only work at a few select stores, making the risk lower. These store cards may offer certain perks, such as promotional notices, special discounts, or exclusive sales. Other co-branded Master credit cards are offered by large retailers and can be used anywhere outside the retail stores.

A secured credit card is a type of credit card in which the cardholder is secured using a security deposit. These cards give limited credit lines equal in value to the respective security deposits and are often refunded after a proven track record of responsible card usage is provided. Secured credit cards are highly sought after by people with poor or limited credit card history. A prepaid debit card is a type of secured credit card where the funds available tally with the money that has already been linked to a bank account. Unsecured credit cards do not need collateral or security deposits. They also offer higher credit lines and lower interest rates in comparison to secured cards.

Benefits of Using Credit Cards

As stated earlier, credit cards do come with benefits. This is why many people tend to get comfortable with them. Credit is a great way to upgrade your finances. With benefits ranging from acquiring better financial products to saving money on interest, the advantages are usually quite attractive. Credit can be a highly valuable asset, even though many people have been negatively affected by their credit scores. That is why changing your mindset and making better financial decisions will allow you to use credit to your advantage and not merely use it as a never-ending stream of money. The big issue with credits is in management; if responsibly and adequately managed, credit cards can be of great value to you. Here are some advantages of using credit cards:

- **Save on interest rates and fees**

A very significant benefit of credit is saving money. For example, in purchasing a home, credit can save you hundreds or even thousands on a mortgage loan. Private student loans, auto loans, credit cards, and credit lines usually give reduced interest rates for people who have a good credit score. So, make sure to set yourself up with a good credit score by paying your debts on time and fully, and you may be able to save on some of your assets.

- **Manage your cash flow**

You don't have to make payments instantaneously when you make a purchase using a credit card. When you swipe your card, the bank holds the money and allows you to make the payments later. Therefore, there is no need to pay interest on the purchases you made as you can pay the entire balance in full when the money is due. This is referred to as a good credit habit, so make sure you make your payments on time. Generally, there is an interval of three weeks from the date of purchase to pay the remaining amount.

- **Avoid utility deposits**

If you are looking to buy a house, rent an apartment, buy a car, or even purchase a cell phone, companies will look at your credit score. If your credit score is below the company's rating standard, then you will have to deposit the money into their account. However, having a strong credit history can help you keep your money in a bank account instead of with the company.

- **Better credit card rewards**

With credit cards that offer travel rewards or cash back, you get roughly 1-5% from every purchase you make. Gaining access to the rewards on credit cards highlighted is impossible with a bad credit score. You can get access to the rewards on the purchases you make when your credit score is good.

- **Emergency fund backup plan**

According to a 2015 Bank of Montreal survey, 56 percent of Canadians say they have less than $10,000 in available emergency funds, 44 percent have less than $5,000, and 21 percent have less than $1,000. Since most bills ranging from car repairs to medical bills are a little above $400, having a credit card can be convenient. It also serves as a good backup plan. Usually, most people have an emergency fund, which can help take care of about three to six months of expenses. Using credit means that if your emergency fund is a little short, you won't be left up a creek without a paddle. You will still be able to pay for an emergency even if you don't have access to that money immediately.

- **Avoid and limit financial fraud**

Cybercrime is an unfortunate reality of the world we live in, especially on debit cards. The possibility of fraud on credit cards is much more limited. If an unauthorized purchase is made on your credit card, it can be wiped off from your statement. Credit cards come with $0 liability for fraudulent transactions and provide more options for fraud protection.

- **Purchase and travel protections**

Most of the best credit cards available provide automatic insurance on each purchase. Instead of paying for expensive coverage from your retailer, you can depend on extended warranty coverage from your credit card. This saves a lot of money when traveling and is sometimes a prerequisite when applying for an international visa. Credit cards often offer trip delay or accident benefits, rental car insurance advantages, and many other benefits that can help you save money.

- **The power of good credit**

Having good credit can save you thousands of dollars when used correctly. Poorly managed credit can rapidly become a difficult-to-manage or expensive task. This is why it is essential to read through your credit score or credit report. The good news is that even if you have bad credit right now, you can build it over time to gain access to the desired accounts. If you settle down and take time to master your credit, you will enjoy the benefits of having a credit card.

The Dangers of Credit Card Debt and How to Avoid Them

Credit cards can be dangerous, specifically for new users who are excited about the idea of now having access to money in advance. Apart from the newbies, even the most experienced users fall into credit card traps. To develop and maintain better credit card habits, you need to understand the dangers that come with credit card use. There are also ways to use credit cards responsibly and evade the common traps that catch many customers. I will explore the pitfalls and their solutions so you can have a stable and beneficial relationship with your credit card. So, make sure you avoid these credit card catastrophes:

- **The temptation to overspend**

It has been discovered that most customers spend much more with credit cards than with cash. In a study, most participants were willing to spend two times the amount with credit cards than with cash. It is relatively easy to spend money using credit cards where the 'pain' of money leaving your pocket is not felt. This explains why there is a high rate of credit card debt. Based on how much you can afford each month, set a limit for your credit card even if it is way below the credit limit. This limit will help you stay on track and avoid racking up large expenses that you probably don't need. Ensure that your lifestyle is not based on impressing people with what you have but is focused on providing yourself and your family with the necessary goods and services for survival and reasonable enjoyment.

- **Interest makes it harder to pay off the balance**

Making payments for credit card balances every month helps you to prevent paying any interest whatsoever. The amount of time needed to pay off the balance is increased if you don't consistently pay your balance in full, and a portion goes to interest payments. Make full payments of your balance to prevent paying any interest.

- **Risk of falling into debt**

Each time you borrow money, you go into debt. As you keep borrowing without repaying, you fall deeper into that debt until paying it back feels impossible. As discussed, debt can lead to more problems than just financial issues. It is much harder to reach your other financial goals when you are knee-deep in debt. Money spent on settling debt makes less money available for other important things like saving for your children's college fund or retirement. To pay those bills, you might have to remain in an unfulfilling job or delay your family goals. Be aware of the signs and keep an eye on your credit balance. If you can feel yourself spiraling out of control, stop. Take a second, reevaluate the situation, and make sure you pay your debt as soon as possible.

- **Risk of ruining your credit score**

Credit cards can majorly impact your credit score. If you make use of your credit card wisely, then you will be able to reap the benefits of a good credit score. However, if you mistakenly miss a payment for a month or more, it can send a shock to your credit score. Minimizing your credit applications, keeping your balance below 30% of your usual credit limit, and paying on time are effective ways to boost your score.

- **Minimum payments create a false sense of security**

To help you pay off your debts, credit card companies usually give you the option of a minimum payment. This means that if your debt is $1000 for the month and you can only pay $500, your credit score won't suffer too much because you are technically paying the debt. However, while you might have paid $500, the minimum payment is actually only $50. Some people fall into the trap of paying the bare minimum and end up racking up an unmanageable amount of debt. Ultimately, you may as well not be paying the debt at all if you are going to stick to paying the minimum amount every month. If you make only the minimum payments, you will spend more time paying your balance and end up paying more interest. The most advisable way to clear off your balance is by paying in full and on time.

- **Confusing credit card terms**

Although credit card terms have become much clearer, there is still a lot of confusion regarding credit card offers. A single credit card can have several interest rates, and knowing which ones apply to you can be unclear. Several consequences can ensue from misunderstanding your credit card terms, for example, increased interest rates and increased fees can damage your credit. Ensure you understand the applicable interest rates and the different kinds of balances you have on your credit. Know what purchases give rewards by reading through your rewards program. Meet with your customer service liaison if you have any questions regarding your credit card.

- **Harder to track spending, especially across multiple credit cards**

The basis for a healthy financial life is the ability to track your spending, and having too many credit cards can make tracking your family's spending difficult. When you use multiple credit cards, you have to keep track of multiple accounts in order to track your expenses, and this can get confusing. You can do this manually in a journal and make use of personal finance software like Quicken or Mint which will be discussed in further detail later in the book.

- **Credit cards come with the risk of credit card fraud**

Everyone is at risk of being a credit card fraud victim. A criminal can steal your credit card or its information from a company you shopped with. The good news is that your liability for fraudulent credit card purchases is restricted. Still, you must report the charges quickly. Monitor your credit card more often and make a report of suspicious charges or missing credit quickly.

As you can see, credit cards can be a double-edged sword. They come with numerous benefits as well as dangers if you are not careful. But, if you are making appropriate financial choices, and you are confident in your ability to manage your money successfully, they can be an asset to your financial strategy. However, at the start of your journey, it is important to focus on your family values and make sure you are not adding extra debt to your load. So, while you are still figuring things out and trying to become financially stable, try to avoid using your card or postpone getting a credit card for the time being.

Chapter 5

Effective Methods to Begin Paying off Your Debt

"There are no shortcuts when it comes to getting out of debt."

—Dave Ramsey

The sad thing about having debt is that it never seems to go away. No matter how hard you save, you always seem to be in the red. The reality is you are not the first, and you certainly won't be the last person to struggle with debt. It is one thing to know the upsides of being debt-free and another to figure out how to become debt-free. The good thing is that there are effective resources that can help you become debt-free. So, to help you through your struggles and difficulties, here are several effective methods for debt repayment so that you can get yourself on track and start living a debt-free life.

- Begin by tallying your debt and then deciding on a timeline for the repayment.
- Incorporate debt repayment in your budget and set aside a particular sum every month to pay off your debt.
- Your debt repayment should be prioritized after you budget for your family's basic essentials such as food, shelter, transportation, utilities, and medication.
- Look for ways to accelerate your repayment. You can try debt snowflaking, which means looking for extra amounts of cash to offset your debt monthly.
- If you owe multiple debts, there is the option of getting a loan consolidation plan for your debt to help cut down

the interest and make payments simpler. However, you should do you research to ensure you only work with reputable companies.
- Compare the snowball and avalanche debt repayment methods (discussed below), which tackle your debt as quickly as possible by taking your extra money and using it to pay off remaining debt.
- Try seeking help from a professional source if you are in a very desperate situation.
- Try negotiating with your creditors to cut down on the outstanding balance you owe them.

The two most useful methods are known as the snowball debt repayment method and the avalanche debt repayment method. These two tactics are very commonly used and incredibly successful when it comes to paying off debt. They can be used for all types of loans, including personal loans, student loans, car loans, and credit card balances.

The Avalanche Method of Debt Repayment

Earlier I told you to start small. However, if you are going to use the avalanche method, then you will probably have to do the exact opposite of that. It works by asking you to identify which of your debts have the highest interest rates. Naturally, you want to pay those off first so that you don't end up paying way more than you need to in interest. So, once you have identified those debts, you begin paying them off. Once that debt has been settled, you move onto the second-highest interest accruing debt. That seems pretty basic, right? But how are you going to pay them off? It's going to take forever! It might take longer; however, the trick with the avalanche method is to pay off the minimum amount for all of your debts in the month. Once you have paid the minimum amounts, you go to the debt with the highest interest rate and pay it off more. In other words, all of your debt will slowly start melting off, with the high-interest debts melting off the fastest. This method is incremental, but before you know it, your debts will be strategically paid off, and you will have saved on interest. For example, imagine you have three credit cards with different balances and varying interest rates:

- Credit Card X – Balance: $1,600, Minimum Payment: $100, Interest Rate: 26%
- Credit Card Y – Balance: $1,000, Minimum Payment: $30, Interest Rate: 23%
- Credit Card Z – Balance: $700, Minimum Payment: $50, Interest Rate: 21%

Using the avalanche method of paying debt, you will begin by making the minimum payments on all the cards. Next, you will pay $250, for instance, towards the credit card with the highest interest rate, which is card X in the above scenario. Once you pay off card X's debt, you move on to card Y, which has the next highest interest rate and repeat the process. After card Y, you tackle card Z, which has the lowest interest rate. This method relieves you of financial pressure and makes sure that you are making headway in paying off your debt and becoming financially stable.

Benefits of the avalanche method of debt payment

- You get to save more money on interest by attacking the debt with higher interest rates first.
- The avalanche method helps you settle your debt faster. Targeting one debt at a time and making large payments will help you clear up debt a lot more efficiently.

Disadvantages of the avalanche method of debt payment

- Depending on how much the debt with the highest interest rate is, it might take a long time to pay off.

- If you cannot afford to make minimum payments monthly, it might feel like you are making little progress and this can be quite discouraging. Although the method can be slow, it is effective. Be patient and keep making the necessary payments.

The Snowball Method of Debt Repayment

In this method, you make minimum payments on all your debt first, just like the avalanche method. However, the main difference is that you begin by paying off the debt with the smallest balance instead of the highest interest rate. In this way, the snowball method is more concerned with balances than with interest rates. Keeping with our earlier credit card examples, you have:

- Credit Card X – Balance: $1,600, Minimum Payment: $100, Interest Rate: 26%

- Credit Card Y – Balance: $1,000, Minimum Payment: $30, Interest Rate: 23%

- Credit Card Z – Balance: $700, Minimum Payment: $50, Interest Rate: 21%

In the snowball method, you begin with credit card Z. After making the minimum payments; you start directing extra monthly payments to credit card Z, which is the credit card with the lowest balance. Once you finish paying off credit card Z, you can move on to credit card Y, repeat the process and finish off with credit card X, which has a balance of $1,600, making it the highest amount owed. In this way, you can systematically eliminate your debts. It's kind of like when you had homework at school. Some kids would tackle the math homework before they moved onto something easier and other kids would finish all the easy homework before they moved onto the harder math homework. The effectiveness of the snowball and avalanche methods are the same; you just have to decide which one suits your family's lifestyle better.

Benefits of the snowball method of debt repayment

- Focusing on the debt with the smallest balance helps you use less money to make more significant strides.

- You get motivated by canceling out your debt, and because you are beginning with your small balances, this is relatively easy to do.

Disadvantages of the snowball method of debt repayment

- You do not avoid paying interest as you would with the avalanche method. This is a disadvantage because you will begin paying off the small debt first, causing the larger ones to accumulate. This accumulation means you will pay more money when you get to the debt with higher interest.

According to research in human behavior and social science, many people find it easier to stay motivated if they tackle the debt that has a smaller balance first. Even though it is rational to want to save more money, people find the snowball method a lot easier than the avalanche method. However, there is no one-size-fits-all for finances. It is up to you to decide what works best for you.

Other Strategies to Begin Repaying Your debt

- **Begin by totaling your debt.**

As soon as you decide on a repayment method that works for you, sum up your debt so that you can identify your interest rates, fees, terms, and balances. You can download a money management app to help you get a comprehensive view of your debt. The most important thing is figuring out which debt you should tackle first. Figuring out where to start will require you to have a holistic understanding of your financial situation. Just like how you made a map for your family values, you have to make a map of your debt. Figure out where you are and where you want to go.

- **As soon as you pay off your debt, start saving.**

The moment you pay off your debt, start saving towards your new goals. You might want to celebrate by spoiling yourself and spending all of your money with a debt-free attitude. Don't do this. Learning how to make better financial decisions will be an ongoing commitment to yourself and your family that you have to uphold. And no, you don't have to live like this for the rest of your life, but you do have to make sure you are in a comfortable position and spending your money instead of saving it will make it easier to fall back into a debt-hole. Use the family values you set up to stay on track and make sure you're not indulging in instant gratification and overspending.

- **Track your progress.**

Maybe you are someone who enjoys making lists, or perhaps you rely on your phone to keep track of meetings and schedules. Maybe you are creative and enjoy making diagrams and maps. However, if you choose to do it, make sure you track your progress. Not only will this keep you motivated, but it will also keep you on the right track. Download apps or use a journal. Keeping track of how your debt is progressing will also allow you to decide which method of debt repayment suits you best. Maybe you try something subconsciously one month, and it ends up being really effective. If you don't keep track of this, you might not know what helped you pay your debts so effectively on that occasion. Pretend it's a recipe. Sometimes inspiration strikes, and you add a few extra spices that you usually wouldn't add. Your family is in awe of the meal you prepared and want to know how you made it. You try recalling the recipe but find that you have forgotten the secret ingredients. Don't let your financial strategy be like that one-hit-wonder of a meal. Take note and see what works best for you.

- **Try to pay more.**

You should always aim to pay as much of your debts as possible. However, sometimes it is difficult because you are only ever able to contribute the minimum payments. In these cases, try to save and cut down as much as possible, just until you get those debts paid off. The more you pay off your loans, the faster you will be debt-free.

- **Save more, spend less.**

People usually have long lists of stuff they want to have, even though they might not be earning enough to afford them all. If you buy everything according to your wants, you might end up running into debt. If you ask very wealthy people, they cannot even afford to buy everything that crosses their minds. The higher your income, the more things you will want, naturally. This is because you have access to more. However, living beyond your means will get you into trouble. Be conscious of what you need versus what you want. If you have some extra money after you paid off your debts and contributed to your retirement fund, go buy yourself that beautiful item, without going into debt, if it makes you happy. The trick is to live within your means and set yourself up for the future.

- **Try downsizing.**

Instead of buying a brand-new car, perhaps a used car might relieve some pressure from your financial situation. Many dealerships offer reasonably priced second-hand cars. At the end of the day, you are buying a car to serve a purpose. You need it to get you places and transport things, so there really is no need to spend an extra $20,000 because a new car might look a bit nicer. Buying a used car in good condition can save you some money. When you are trying to pay off your debt, you need to take advantage of all the avenues that can help you save money. While buying a used car is a productive first step, one should also remember to make sure that the car is fuel-efficient and in good condition. You don't want to end up spending thousands of dollars just getting it fixed. If the fuel consumption is high, it could bump up your monthly expenses significantly.

Alternatively, you could avoid buying a car and use alternative methods of transport. You can use public transport, walk, ride a bike, or carpool with friends and colleagues. The financial pressure of having cars can create tension and stress, and you might find that having more than one is a bit excessive depending on your family's needs. If you are too far away from work, move closer, and drive less. Perhaps you have to pay a little more in rent or mortgage, but you won't have to pay off a car. Imagine how much money you can save by doing this. Car ownership and maintenance do not come cheap. The cost of these two factors can run into thousands of dollars in a year, money that would be better spent paying off your debt.

Instead of jumping right into getting that second car, try to experiment with one. Cars also have different types of insurance, so to save money, continue with the cheapest insurance plan. You might be thinking about the cost of commuting by bus, train, or taxi, but they don't cost as much as driving or owning a car. Consider the costs of insurance, fuel, and maintenance. You could be saving as much as $800 for every $1000 you would spend on car maintenance and repairs.

- **Save on groceries.**

Buy your groceries in bulk when they are on sale. You don't have to only buy things when you need them. Buy non-perishable and household items if they are on sale so that you don't have to buy them at full price in a few months. This way, you will be saving money that can be used to pay off parts of your debt. Keep track of sales and use coupons where possible. Often, for convenience, it can be easy to stick to one grocery store to source all of your groceries. Yes, it might be convenient, but stores offer a variety of the same goods at different prices. Do your research and figure out which stores have the cheapest versions of the goods you need and buy accordingly.

- **Get another source of income.**

You can try and make more money by picking up extra shifts or working multiple jobs. It's true; not every family is capable of doing this. However, if you are serious about repaying your debt and your current income makes this difficult, finding an extra source of money will help you get into the building wealth mode quicker. The target is not to work more hours but to use money obtained from these side jobs to pay off your debt. If you work more and spend more, then your level of debt will remain the same. So make sure you are using that money to pay off debt and not to live above your means.

It also does not need to be a long-term arrangement. Perhaps you find a side hustle that requires you to work for two weekends a month. In reality, this is a small sacrifice for the prospect of living debt-free. Plus, it's temporary. Another way to make extra money is to monetize your hobbies or skills. For example, if you are great at web designing, you can create websites for businesses online. You can also teach people how to design websites and charge them a fee for your expertise.

- **Rent out a part of your home.**

Maybe you live in a three-bedroom house and use one of the bedrooms as a study room. Consider clearing it out and renting it to a friend or tenant. The money from the rent can be used to pay utilities and contribute to your monthly mortgage or rent, freeing up some money at the end of the month. If you find yourself out of town often, try renting out the space while you are away. This is a great option for families that have a lot of free space in their homes. To take this even further, you can list your homes on platforms like Airbnb to extend your reach and help you make more money.

- **Understand your spending patterns.**

This method works well because we tend to shop and spend without actually thinking about *how* we shop and spend. If you take the time to analyze your expenses, you might be shocked at how much you can save. Understanding why and when you spend can help you identify moments of weakness in your spending habits and handle them instead of spending more money. Keep a purchase journal that outlines when you spent money and how you were feeling. If you notice that you spend more money every time you start to feel overwhelmed by your financial situation or other stressors, you can begin to constructively deal with this impulse and save your money.

- **Get a consolidation loan.**

Some banks allow you to pool all of your debts into one big debt with a lower interest rate. If your bank offers this, your chances of clearing your debt faster will be higher. For this kind of loan to work, you need to make sure you are saving and actively paying off the debt. It is hard to think about saving money when you need to pay off debt, but without it, you will be accruing more debt. A bank in the US found that 70 people out of 100 who took a consolidated loan to pay off their outstanding balances still had debt problems after paying their initial loans. The reason for this is because they did not address their spending habits. They continued to spend more than they earned. For a consolidation loan to work, you need to have a structured budget. It will give you control over whatever money you earn, and you will be able to focus on necessities.

- **Consider refinancing your mortgage.**

Refinancing your mortgage can help pay off your debt. You can sum up all of the loans you want to repay into your mortgage. However, if your home is not worth much, this might not be a good option. Before you take this step, speak to an expert in the field. Try to talk to someone apart from the person you owe because they don't always have your best interests in mind. Speak to a certified counselor in this field. Do not take any offers from money lending companies, especially if your bank is not willing to help you. A certified financial counselor might open your eyes to other options aside from mortgage refinancing. If you choose to work with them, they might be able to help you hit your target. Also, always remember that there will be cases of emergencies. There will be times when you need to spend from your savings, or you will need to borrow. If you borrow too many times using your house as collateral, when you retire, you may be spending your pension to repay these debts.

- **Get financial counseling.**

If you are finding it challenging to stick to your plans, or are unable to decide which debt repayment method is the one for you, speak to a credit counselor. They understand how your bank works and will be able to advise you on the more technical aspects of the services they offer. Speaking to a counselor can offer you clarity and a way forward.

Bringing Debt into a Marriage and How to Deal With it

Marriage can be complicated. It is the union of two individual entities that establish a new institution as one. Each individual has a different background and upbringing that they contribute to the marriage. Everyone has different habits, views, opinions, and ways of being. So, how do you function in a marriage when you and your partner have opposing views on financial management? What if you are really good at saving and paying off debt, but your partner isn't? How do you navigate the complexities of financial matters within a marriage? While you might have to figure out the complexities within the parameters of your own marriage, I can tell you that hiding information is not the place to start. This creates a foundation of distrust and can affect your marriage negatively in the long-term. Surprisingly, bringing debt into a marriage has become a common problem nowadays. Many people have student loans that they still need to pay off and don't want to wait for that to happen before they start living their lives. Seven out of ten Americans enter into marriage with debt. As many of us already know, money issues are the primary cause of divorce in many marriages today. This is because of the central role money plays in an individual's life. There are many issues associated with money. So, how do you clear up the issue of debt with your partner before making a long-term commitment?

One way to avoid money fights in your marriage is to open up to your partner about your finances. Let them know everything about your financial status and/or debt status. If your partner is aware of your financial situation, then you can figure out how to overcome any challenges together. However, if you do not tell your partner about your debt, you will be starting your marriage off with financial dishonesty.

The significance of money in your marriage cannot be overemphasized. It is involved in every crucial shared decision you make. While it would be great to live in a world where money didn't really matter, and all you had to worry about was your love for one another, that is not the world you live in. So, discuss these questions with your partner after carefully considering them. Here are the questions you should be asking your partner when discussing your financial matters:

- Do you have a debt-repayment plan?
- How long will it take you to settle outstanding debts?
- How many credit cards do you own, and what are the balances?
- Do you have any financial responsibilities in your past relationships, like child support?

- How much do you save and spend each month?
- How soon do you pay your bills?
- What is your opinion on credit cards?

Note that you should also be ready to answer these questions after asking your partner. There are usually many financial expenses in marriage. Both partners have various individual needs while there are also needs that apply to both of them. To avoid conflict of interest and wasteful spending, which could later lead to debt, you and your partner should plan together, discuss your debt and find a way forward. Also, consider discussing these questions with your partner:

- Will there be a joint account, or should each person keep their money separate?
- How will you financially support the children you plan on having?
- Do you prefer that both parents work outside the home or do you have a preference for one to stay at home with the kids?
- Are you interested in long-term investments?
- Have you already started a retirement plan?

There are no wrong or right answers to these questions. For instance, your partner may prefer to keep their money separate rather than own a joint account. This is not a bad thing or sign of mistrust. It is a preference and should be treated as such. It is up to you to decide to go ahead with the marriage if you feel you both have common goals and can decide as a couple—hence, why it is important to discuss finances before marriage. Partners who understand each other regarding monetary issues have to quantify their goals. They have to jot down their plans and make formal arrangements that correspond with the money at hand. Couples who run a business-like financial affair are usually happier. They draw out a budget and stick to it; they also track their spending and income and pay bills on time.

How to Teach Children About Finances and Debt

Teaching your Children about Finances

Teaching your kids about finances will help you to figure out what money management means to you as a parent. Your definition of financial management will be a determining factor in how you approach educating your kids. You will be able to easily teach your children how they can save money if you have a better understanding of your own financial behavior.

After you have defined it for yourself and your children, figure out which of your financial habits are good and which ones you should not be teaching or illustrating to your children. For example, instant gratification might be an issue that you deal with and, therefore, have to teach your children about delayed appreciation. This mindset (that you need to wait to enjoy something) is an important aspect of dealing with money. Most people want their children to know that there shouldn't or can't be instant satisfaction for every desire. Working towards and saving for your wants can make achieving them that much more rewarding. This is also an important life lesson to learn because it teaches you to enjoy the journey with them.

So, where do you begin? Here are a few suggestions:

1. **Give your children a piggy bank.** Encourage your children to put any money they receive through chores,

birthdays and other special occasions in the piggy bank. Any time they add more money into the piggy bank they should add up the total amount so they know how much money they have. When your children ask for a treat, you can encourage them to pay for it with the money they've saved up.

2. **Teach them the difference between a need and a want.** Although your children may have some money saved in their savings, they probably won't have enough to buy everything they'd like in the store. This is a good opportunity to get them to understand the difference between saving for a 'need,' something they require like a bike helmet, versus a 'want,' which is something they desire, such as a pair of premium earbuds. It's important to teach your children that the needs should be saved and paid for first and then save for the wants after the needs are taken care of.

3. **Include your children in real-life spending decisions.** When you're at the grocery store with your children, involve them in your food choice process. Go to the store with a spending budget for the family groceries and let them help you stay within the budget. If the shopping cart items seem like they will be over the budget, start picking out what can be removed and purchased next time around. Show them how they can save money by looking for sales and imparting what you consider to be a good value for a product.

4. **Let your children contribute money to important purchases.** If your teen asks for a car, propose the idea of paying for a portion of the vehicle's cost. If your child has a part-time job or has money saved

up, it will be a good learning opportunity for them to go through the experience of feeling the emotional friction that takes place when buying a bigger ticket item. It will help them be aware of the value of the car, other fees, and costs associated with the purchase of the car and hopefully display more responsibility when taking care of it.

5. **Set up a bank account for your children.** As soon as you open a bank account for them, they will start learning the value of making sure money is available anytime they require it. A monthly account statement is essential because it displays a little interest payment at the top of the page, and this is a good lesson in the appreciation or depreciation of money. While your child's bank account balance increases, explain to them why and how this can prevent them from financial hardship and gives them the purchasing power to decide how they can spend. You can also show them the disadvantage of having an empty bank account.

By showing them how interest rates work, you can show them how borrowing money will give the lender more money due to interest payments. Also, let them know that debt can be dangerous because of that very reason. The moment your child starts mastering arithmetic, you can begin to teach them about budgeting. Use tools and games to better their understanding of budgets and money. For example, you can use colorful cups to represent monthly expenses, and candy can be used as money. Show them that some money goes to a car loan, some to a mortgage. Teach them about rent and groceries, and then use some extra candy to teach them about saving. Children learn through stories and anecdotes so try not to get too technical. Try to make it fun!

As soon as your child has an understanding of what a budget is, encourage them to create a budget for themselves. If you offer the child an allowance, tell them to save some of the allowance money in their bank account before making use of the remaining amount for leisure purchases. Review the budget together and make sure to communicate about how and why they set up the budget the way they did.

There are vital lessons that can be learned from a child's bank account, and the most important thing is the interest payments. In the next steps, you need to explain the way interest flows in both inward and outward directions. The inward direction is anytime you save, while the outward direction is when you run the balance on your credit card or take out a loan. Make sure your child knows the reason lenders collect interest and the reason interest rates on unsecured debit or credit cards are more than on a car or house loan than collateral loans.

It is advisable you also let them know the tools creditors use anytime they make decisions on credit. Even though you aren't required to go into detail on how they derive credit scores (many adults don't understand this either), you can tell them that to pay off balances anytime they are due is the most effective way to getting a good credit score.

Lastly, teach them about the risks of debt. If something terrible happens like an expensive car repair, medical emergency, or unemployment, you should have enough savings to continue to live comfortably. There should be emergency funds set aside by your family for covering the mortgage, food, and utilities if you happen to lose your job or become ill.

Sharing your financial story

When your children are old enough, you may want to involve them in conversations regarding money. They want to be independent beings, but they are still financially dependent on you. This is a good time to teach them about your financial story, your financial history and your situation. For example, the basics of your mortgage details or your car loan terms or a breakdown of your monthly bills, the types of investments you have. You don't have to give them every single detail but the information you provide should give them a sense of structure as to how things work.

As soon as they turn 18, your children will get credit offers from banks, department stores, and other retailers. Because of your careful dedication to their financial intelligence and savvy, they will go into the world and make the right financial decisions. You can assist them in learning how they can handle credit cards by letting them sign up for secured credit cards that limit spending to between $250 – $500. When they pay off little amounts monthly and avoid late fees and interest, they will understand how useful credit cards can be if used responsibly.

Learning about Debt

Debt is one of the most prevalent issues in our society today and it all starts with your upbringing. A child raised in a home where debt is brushed off and accepted will increase the chance of that child finding themselves in debt in their adult life. Children are like sponges and if you, as a parent, are not good at saving or handling money, they will adopt your method of managing finances and, in essence, create a new generation of financial mismanagement. It is crucial to teach your children effective financial management principles. Teach them to be prudent, to save more, to live within a budget, and avoid debt at all costs. Let them know the dangers of depending on borrowed money. This is crucial to building generational wealth.

Similarly, teach your kids how to manage debt before they find themselves in it. Talk to them about borrowing and the hidden costs they may incur as they move through life. Set up interesting live-action games that will help them gain the decision-making skills necessary for handling finances. Even if you have a history of debt, try to make sure that your children do not fall into the same traps. Don't treat money as a taboo.

Another lesson you should consider discussing with your kids is the kinds of debt. Some argue that debt is-debt-is debt. Others argue that there is good debt and bad debt. Regardless of your opinion on this debate, it would be useful for your children to understand why there is a distinction made between the two.

What is Good vs. Bad Debt?

Good debt deals with investments. Anytime you purchase a house, you are both buying shelter and paying for an asset that tends to appreciate in value as time goes on. It might take years for you to finish paying off a house loan, but when the equity increases and the house value grows, it can be a great investment. Expensive cars, fine dining, and travel will likely bring temporary enjoyment but have no positive impact on your net worth. In a situation where you get them by borrowing money, they can result in significant debt with no financial returns. This would be an example of bad debt.

Your children should know the differences between bad debt and good debt. It's your responsibility to teach your kids how they can save money for emergencies, significant purchases, and more importantly, retirement. It would be beneficial for them to understand that their life goals can be undermined by acquiring unnecessary debt. Your kids should know that outstanding debt shouldn't be taken lightly. They must keep to their promises if they have decided to pay the debt, and failure to do so may result in legal, financial, and personal repercussions.

Mini-loan Exercise

You can show your children the concept of debt by giving them a small loan on things they want but can't afford to buy. For example, if your 12-year-old wants a new book and they want to buy it but don't have enough money, you can turn this into a teaching moment. Tell them you will give them a loan but they have to pay it back within three months. Every time a payment is late, add more money to the loan. By doing so, your child will begin to understand the concept of debt and how to manage it. Instead of spending their money on sweets as they normally would, they save it and use it to pay you for the book. Now, you don't have to do this all the time, but doing it every once in a while, will allow them to grasp financial matters and set them up for the future.

Paying for college

Another necessary conversation you'll likely have with the older children pertaining to debt is in regards to student loans for college. Going to college has never been more expensive than it is today. Without intentional and long-term savings, many families can't afford to pay their children's tuition fees without going into debt. There are many kinds of student loans available and they each offer different repayment periods and interest rates. It would be prudent for you to walk through the student loan process with your children and the subsequent responsibilities related to paying it back as quickly as possible.

That being said, there are other methods to pay for your child's college and university education if you plan ahead. Both the U.S. and Canada offer programs parents should consider participating in when saving for their child's education.

- In America, the 529 plan is a tax-advantaged savings plan designed to help you pay for education. 529 plans are tax-advantaged accounts that can be used to cover educational expenses from kindergarten through graduate school.
- In Canada, a Registered Education Savings Plan or RESP is a special savings account for parents who want to save for their child's education after high school. RESPs are also tax-advantaged accounts. The Canadian government pays investors of the program to save by contributing a grant of up to $7,200 over the life of the plan.
- For both the U.S. and Canadian programs, the primary benefit is that there are no taxes on cash withdrawals if they go toward qualified educational expenses.
- Applying for scholarships, bursary awards and co-op work terms are also very popular options for students to help pay for tuition, accommodations and/or course materials.
- And of course, many students also work part-time jobs on or off campus to supplement the high cost of school related expenses.

So, regardless of the methods you choose to pay for your child's education, the best tip I can advise is to start planning early.

Chapter 6

Saving Money for Rainy Days

> "All days are not the same. Save for a rainy day. When you don't work, savings will work for you."
>
> —M.K. Soni

One of the most effective routes to creating wealth still comes down to saving money. Once upon a time saving money included stashing physical money into "piggy banks" or underneath mattresses. People didn't have to save as much money because inflation rates were low and money had more value 50 years ago. You could buy a house for a few hundred dollars instead of a few hundred thousand dollars. Times have changed and emergency funds are essential to your future well-being. It can be easy to brush these things off. *Why do I need a rainy day fund? Why can't I just spend the money I worked so hard to earn?* Well, because life is unpredictable and you never know what could happen. You could lose your job tomorrow or get into a terrible accident that leaves you unable to work and with a mountain of medical bills. Unfortunate events happen to people every day and you need to make sure you are financially prepared for any event.

What Is a Rainy Day Fund?

An emergency fund may be a concept that you are familiar with, but rainy day funds are a little different. A rainy day fund is intended as a safety measure for lower-cost and shorter-term troubles, like parking tickets and home maintenance. Their scope and size are the major difference between a rainy day fund and an emergency fund. A rainy day fund is dedicated to the smaller but more anticipated expenses that may come your way. Everyone expects these inconveniences and they are not usually so severe.

On the contrary, an emergency fund is to be used for completely unexpected life events, such as job loss, new sports equipment, a new roof or any other event with serious implications on your finances. It's good practice to be intentional about saving for rainy days. It can be stressful to live paycheck to paycheck. It can also be nerve-racking knowing that having to take time off work due to falling ill could lead you to severe financial insecurity. In these scenarios, having to deal with unexpected or even expected expenses can lead to having to borrow money or even defaulting on payments in the worst case.

Saving gives you financial security and protection from unexpected events. Believe it or not, saving also makes you happier. In a study conducted by the Northwestern Mutual Insurance Company, they found that savings are connected to happiness. In reality, researchers suggest that people who are "forecasters" and are executing future-based actions, like making investments and setting financial goals, feel much better and happier about their lifestyles than other people who are not making conscious efforts to settle and achieve their financial objectives.

On a similar note, the Consumer Federation of America demonstrated a direct relationship between longer lifespans and savings. Specifically, those who have budget proposals are far more likely to have reserved funds for emergencies and are far less susceptible to anxiety and stress disorders. These findings make a lot of sense, given that not saving money can result in a greater level of tension that can later create chronic health problems if not addressed.

What expenses do you anticipate that your family will have? Think about all the areas or items that require a small fix—like the need to purchase another battery for your car or the need to get a new mattress for your bed. These types of expenses are what your rainy day funds are meant to cover. A savings account that you dedicate to a rainy day does not necessarily have to be a very big one with lots of money.

Coming to terms with the appropriate figure to save in your rainy-day fund account requires a personal evaluation of the unforeseen events that may occur in your family and their potential costs. For instance, if you have a house, you may need more money to replace some worn out or broken appliances such as an air conditioning unit, a boiler, or a driveway. Or maybe your child has a school trip that requires a fee to participate. Having a rainy day fund may be what you need if someone in your family gets sick and has to visit a doctor or if one of your children sprains their ankle. As much as you take the necessary precautions to ensure that you cushion the drastic effect of some rainy days, you also want to make sure that you set up a rainy day fund account that you can easily access.

For a rainy day fund, you want your cash to be accessible. Look out for a money market savings account that will provide you with some level of interest and let you withdraw your cash at very short notice without having to deliberate much on the status of the market. Just because you had an expense pop up out of the blue does not mean that you have to let it affect your locked-in longer-term savings accounts and investments. Leave those alone! Instead, compare money market and high-yield savings accounts if you are interested in looking for a place to keep your family's rainy day money.

Studies showing that people experiencing a feeling of control over the events of their lives cope better and are more adaptable to unpredictable situations. Similarly, individuals are especially dissatisfied in circumstances when they deem themselves unable to control the situation. Therefore, having a rainy day fund will prevent these feelings of frustration and allow you to feel more secure despite unexpected changes. Now, let us look into some of the reasons why saving for a rainy day is important for you and your family.

- **It could serve as a cushion if you lose your job.**

It does not matter if you have a high level of job security in your workplace; when it comes to employment, just about anything can happen. Having sufficient funds to cater to expenses and bills for at least half a year is a wise decision. This is important because it will provide you with ample time to cushion the adverse effects of the situation you find yourself in until you can find another source of income.

- **You may become seriously ill and not be able to work.**

Because these expenses are difficult to foresee, they can be harder to save for. For this reason, it is very important that you set some funds aside for rainy days, even if it feels futile. You never know what could happen and of course, we hope it won't!

- **A costly home repair may arise.**

Sometimes your roof starts leaking, and the water stops running hot. Sometimes your kids break something important when playing around. You aren't in control of what happens, and having some extra money put aside for this specific purpose will allow you to maintain financial stability and maintain the fixes in your house. If you have home insurance, replacing appliances or repairing the damage may not be too challenging for you. But it is also important to note that your home insurance isn't going to pay for all the costs. To this end, you will need to withdraw some funds from your rainy day account.

- **Your car may break down.**

It is easy to take a vehicle for granted, especially if it does not break down frequently. But the truth is that for every mile you drive, the likelihood of your car breaking down increases. There are some scenarios where the total amount you need to repair your car is as small as $50. But in some other cases, you may even need thousands of dollars to finance the repair of your vehicle.

Some Simple Methods to Save For a Rainy Day

- **Put all your passive change in a jar/automate small bank transfers.**

If you receive change from a store, don't spend it directly after you get it. Put it in a jar and promise that you won't use what is in the jar for one whole year. At the end of the year, you will be surprised how much you have saved. Similarly, some banks have an automated function for their accounts to move small amounts of money as 50 cents from your checking account to your saving whenever a charge has been made. Collecting such small funds, even if it may appear insignificant at first, will eventually grow to be sufficient for addressing some of your emergency needs. Though it may not be easy at the start, with some practice and perseverance, you will have enough money saved up in no time.

- **Make your coffee by yourself.**

Rather than stopping at a café and buying one, you may want to start making your own coffee. When you do that, channel the money you would have used to buy the coffee into your rainy day account. With time, you will be surprised that the amount in your rainy day funds account will skyrocket. It doesn't only have to be coffee. Look at the small purchases you make on a daily basis. Do you buy breakfast or lunch from a restaurant instead of making your own? Depending on your lifestyle, figure out what you are buying and what you can do yourself. Save that money and start contributing to your rainy day fund.

- **Use your points to redeem free gift cards or cash-back bonuses.**

When you use the gift card at your favorite restaurant or store, take the real money you would have spent from your checking account and place it into your interest-bearing savings account instead. You would have spent the money anyway, so you might as well earn some interest on it.

- **Convert your reward points or credit card bonus into cash.**

Many debit and credit card service providers are now offering reward points to customers who use their cards every day. You want to make sure that you are part of such programs so that you can have some benefits whenever you make a purchase. Take that money and save it for a rainy day! Sometimes they offer deals for a specific shop and you may be tempted to buy something you don't need just because you have the points. If you convert these points to cash, you can avoid making unnecessary purchases and save money instead.

The Importance of Emergency Funds

A research study conducted in 2018 showed that a whopping 57% of Americans are scared of being broke in the future. The same study stated that about 53% confessed that they are anxious about being stuck with huge health bills. This makes a lot of sense because roughly 66% of Americans attribute their financial instability to health expenses. Only 39% of Americans have the necessary funds to make up for a one-thousand-dollar emergency. It is now glaringly obvious why building your emergency fund is very important for your fiscal health.

An emergency fund is very important because it acts like a financial safety vest that will make you relatively secure without having to opt for loans or depend on your credit card. If you run into debt now and then, an emergency fund might be just what you need to keep you from running deeper into debt. It has been said that a very effective way of coming out of debt is to avoid getting into it. So, how can an emergency fund help you?

- **It helps with unforeseen medical expenses.** In the U.S., health insurance is very important in easing the brunt of your medical expenses. Although your health insurance policy may cater to routine and general medical checkups, the policy may not cater to hospital visits, ambulance rides, and specific procedures.

- **It cushions the financial implications of a job loss.** While job security may mean that your chances of being laid-off are slimmer, the truth is that there is no true job security anywhere. So, just in case having an emergency fund will give you some breathing room to find another job. The cash accrued in your emergency funds account needs to be sufficient to cater to you and your family members.

If saving for six months' worth of living costs is overwhelming, start small, and set a three-month goal. Increase your savings each month, and put in extra money such as bonuses, income tax refunds, and gifts. Take the giant leap and make plans for the amount of money that you will need to survive, and then go ahead and create a budget to that effect. It may be somewhat overwhelming to start saving huge amounts of money, so saving for short periods should be your priority in the beginning.

- **It pays for unexpected home and car repairs.** Over time, as a car and homeowner, some expenditures are necessary. Although many people turn to their car and home insurance to bridge the gaps in these emergency costs, not all are covered by insurance policies. You will have to be prepared to spend out-of-pocket, as with healthcare coverage.

How Much Do You Need for Your Emergency Fund?

When you consider drafting a budget for your emergency funds account, it is important to consider the amount of money you need to lead a life of comfort. As stated before, professionals will often advise you to have an amount of cash that can serve your family for at least one year. You will need to draft your family's income and monthly spending in order to come up with a monthly figure that you can multiply by six or twelve. The multiplied amount will be an adequate amount of money to keep in your emergency funds.

Funds may be hard for you to get; in this case, you need to start small. Saving about 10% of your emergency funds account is a very wise step. Each time you have extra cash like income tax refunds, bonuses, or pay raises, consider saving it in your emergency fund account. When you are starting out, begin with a definite objective and a concrete number in your mind. This will ensure that you have a goal that you want to achieve, instead of just passively convincing yourself that you need to save. Also, have the timeframe in your mind. How long do you want to save? When you find the answer to this question, calculate the amount of time that it will take you to accomplish this. Remember those SMART goals! Irrespective of the amount that you earn, it is always within your power to come up with a customized plan to begin saving for your emergency fund account and reach your objective. So, how can you start saving for an emergency fund?

Reduce Your Spending

Drastically reducing unnecessary spending is the first step that you need to take when you want to start building an emergency fund account. This singular act can make more money available to your family, giving you the room to increase the leftover amount after the payment of your monthly bills. Also, you can reduce expenses when you make a conscious decision to cut back on dining out, toys, shopping, vacations, entertainment, and unsubscribing from unimportant services. Evaluate your monthly subscriptions, bills, and expenditures and consciously check out what you can eliminate or reduce. If you intend to take more drastic steps to increase your savings every month, put the following into consideration:

- **Relocate to a cheaper area.** This option is particularly less stressful for people renting a place. Your rent is likely your most expensive expense which means that you will be saving a lot of cash when you find a way to reduce it.

- **Sell your car.** You may want to take public transportation, particularly if you stay in an area where there is a reliable public transit system. If you have two cars in your household, try selling one of them and share the other one with the rest of your family members. The funds gained from selling a car may be enough to start a significant emergency fund.

- **Discard your storage unit.** One out of every eleven Americans pays about $91 every month for storage. The industry is worth a staggering $38 billion. Instead of storing all of your old stuff, sell it and put that money into an emergency fund.

- **Find a side hustle.** Making money from a side hustle is becoming increasingly popular. About one in three Canadians has a side business. Recent investigations have concluded that having a side hustle is an effective way to earn more money.

Where Should You Keep Your Emergency Fund?

Similar to your rainy day savings account, you should keep your emergency fund in a savings account that you can easily access, preferably with a very high-interest rate. This account must be very accessible because an emergency can strike without any prior notice. But you should strive to separate the account from your everyday bank account. This will help you to avoid the temptation of digging into your reserves.

How Do You Build Your Emergency Fund Account?

1. **Estimate the amount of money that you intend to save.** Have a clear objective even before you start. When you do this, it will become a habit and less taxing to do.

2. **Save the change.** After buying something with cash, you will likely get a few $5 and $1 bills; make sure that you save this in your money jar. Transfer it to your savings account when the jar becomes full and start earning interest on your money. These tips may be repetitive, but they work.

3. **Save your tax refund.** You'll benefit from a tax refund once every year during tax season, and it is only logical that you make the most of it. One way of doing this is to save it, a super-efficient way to increase your emergency fund balance.

4. **Adjust and assess contributions.** After a few months, check back to see the amount you have been saving and make changes if you need to put more cash into it. It is particularly crucial to do this if you are going through a financially strenuous time, like relocating or getting married. In this case, you need to be cognizant of the money in your emergency funds account and make sure you aren't spending it on the wedding.

Sinking Funds: What are they and How Do they Work?

When financial experts talk about sinking funds, they mean funds that are intentionally reserved for expected and recurring expenses. There are expenses in your budget that you know will be coming up for payment. Instead of waiting for the due date, you can save a portion of each pay and overtime you will have enough saved by the time the due date arrives. Unlike an emergency or rainy day fund which is used for dealing with life's unpredictable emergencies and occurrences, a sinking fund puts you in a better position to pay for your expenses. It is a great way to avoid financial stress especially when you have exhausted your rainy day and emergency funds.

Sinking funds can be set up for your family. Say, for instance, you have established a sinking fund for a family vacation. You can set a goal of $5,000 for the trip you want to take with your family next year. You can then designate $100 each from your paychecks for the year, and by the time you're ready to book the trip, you have the money already set aside in cash. Even if you book the trip on your credit card, you just pay your credit card off immediately afterward. Done and done.

You can set up a sinking fund for any purchase or service you are expecting. You can use them for sports membership fees, school fees, subscriptions, donations; you name it, the possibilities are endless.

But how are sinking funds different from a savings account? Both of these include setting up a sum of cash for the future; however, there is a slight distinction between a savings account and sinking funds. The key distinction is that the latter is built for a specific reason and is to be accessed at a specific time, while the savings account is built for whatever reason it can fulfill.

Why Do You Need a Sinking Fund?

- **To avoid interest charges.** Sinking funds can help you avoid borrowing on a credit card or line of credit that otherwise would have made you pay interest. Interest charges can seem like small and insignificant amounts of money to pay, but they drain you one way or the other in the long-run. Sinking funds help you avoid loans entirely. Loan interest charges are even higher than those of your savings accounts.

- **Your emergency fund will not be touched.** If you do not have sinking funds and you don't want to borrow the money, you might be forced to spend some of your emergency fund. But with sinking funds, you can keep your emergency fund intact for emergencies, not expected expenses.

- **It keeps you intentional.** When you're planning to save up for a known expense, it means that you are being intentional, which is a crucially important factor in becoming financially secure. Financial planning for known expenses reduces the element of surprise when it comes to spending. In other words, you'll be less likely to overspend in July if you already remember that a big expense is due. Having sinking funds forces you to map out your known expenses for the year and not just the month.

How do you Create your Sinking Funds?

There are various ways to start up sinking funds. However, the following tips can help you do it with ease:

1. Open a savings account

You have to open a different bank account for each of your sinking funds, so they do not get mixed up. A savings account is a better option because it yields interest on your deposits and does not charge monthly fees. An online bank is usually a better choice because they offer higher interest. Setting up a savings account will reduce the temptation to take the money out of your checking account and will make you more likely to save. Ideally, you want this account to be liquid so that you can pay off your dues using the money whenever it suits you or whenever a debt arises. Some people prefer to use an envelope system with cash money. With each pay, you allocate the appropriate amount of cash in each designated envelope.

2. Schedule recurring transfers

You can do this monthly by automating your bank account to transfer between one account to the next. It makes it easier to cultivate a healthy saving habit. If your income is low, you can set a smaller amount as your recurring contribution and then do a one-time transfer with your excess income at the end of the month. A sinking fund is very helpful, although not mandatory. If you have sinking funds, you will be able to enjoy their benefits, but if you don't, just make sure you save enough.

Now that you understand the benefits of having enough money to account for emergencies and unexpected events you can begin to incorporate these funds into your monthly budget. Make sure you are saving enough to cover the costs of any emergencies. The rainy day fund will be the quickest to save for while the emergency fund may take a few months before you are in a comfortable financial position. And on the other end of savings accounts, sinking funds keep you alert and aware of the expected expenses that will be coming your way throughout the year. They are all beneficial tools that can help position you and your family for financial security and success. These are tried and true. Give them a try.

Chapter 7

Investing in Your Family's Future

"An investment in knowledge pays the best interest."

—Benjamin Franklin

What does it mean to invest? Investing is the allocation of money with the expectation of making profits. You can invest in assets like real estate (perhaps aiming to sell it at a higher price as the value appreciates) or you can invest in endeavors like starting a business with your money and selling it at a higher price when it increases in value. You can also invest in stocks and shares and make money without having to start your own business.

The central principle of investment is the anticipation of a return in income. While it might seem like a get-rich-quick scheme, investing does come with certain risks. Low-risk investments typically result in low returns, while higher returns are followed by higher-risk investments. Equities or stocks are deemed to be more volatile, with commodities commonly seen as the riskiest investments. It is also possible to invest in land or real estate. In contrast, people may also invest in art and antiques. Paintings by famous artists can certainly appreciate over time. If you are looking to invest, one of the key principles is to make sure you invest in something that will become more valuable. You don't really want to invest in a car because they lose value every time you drive it, but if you are buying a house then it will appreciate in a few years and be worth more than it is when you buy it. Think of investing like interest rates, except better. If you put your money into a savings account in the bank your money earns interest. It is usually not that much but it still appreciates, and that is a good thing. However, when you invest in a house, other factors like the property market and inflation rates will make sure that the house appreciates over time. A two-bedroom that you bought for $250,000 could be worth $700,000 in 40 years.

With regard to stocks, return and risk anticipations differ widely. A stock that lists on the New York Stock Exchange, for instance, would have a more distinct risk-return index in comparison to a smaller stock exchange. The returns that you can receive from stock investments depend on what you invested in. For example, many stocks pay regular dividends (payments made to investors). Bonds usually pay interest every quarter of the year, and rental revenue is generated by real estate. You can either make use of the dividends and interest earned on your investments or you leave it to be reinvested and make you more money. Shares are parts of a business. The business can be private or public. If the business is private then the shares are not open to the general public, however, if it is public, this means you can buy a portion of the business and own that small part of it. A stock refers to the shares you have in that business, while dividends are the money you receive from these shares. Dividends can be reinvested or paid out on a yearly basis (or monthly, depending on the stock). Did you follow all of that? If you didn't, it's okay; investing lingo can be quite technical at first. So, let's delve in a bit deeper to get a better understanding.

Types of Investments

Even though the investment world is vast and somewhat confusing, once you have a handle on the different types of investments you can make you will be able to make an educated and informed decision. I'm sure you have heard many horror stories of investments gone wrong and it can happen. But if you start small and do your research the interest you earn on your investments can help you invest more, pay off your debt and build up your family's wealth. So, what is out there?

Shares

As I said, a share is a part of the business. Think of it like a pie that is divided into eight slices. If you buy one of those slices (but you don't take it home and eat it because it's part of the business) then you own a share of that pie. But why wouldn't you take it home and eat it? Well, because the company may sell it to someone else at a higher price and you would be able to take the difference home. Someone who owns shares in a company is known as a shareholder who benefits from the appreciation of the stock price and frequent dividends received from the earnings of the company. They may contribute to the company's development and progress. Stocks and shares are similar but the main difference is that they refer to different companies. If you have 50 shares of a business then you have invested in one business. However, if you have 50 stocks, that means you have 50 different investments in 50 different companies. There are two types of stock:

- **Common Stock:** With this kind of stock, you have a percentage of ownership in the company. You can vote on things that affect the organization and you can receive dividends.
- **Preferred Stock:** Unlike common stocks, this does not give you the right to vote. However, as an investor in this kind of stock, you can obtain a specific monthly dividend based on the stock price. If you are working and busy then this may be the right stock for you as it requires less time and expertise.

The risks and returns for these stocks differ based on specific factors like the performance of the company, the political and economic scene of the company, and the general state of the economy. However, if you invest in the right thing at the right time and use those factors to guide your investments, you could make a lot of money.

Bonds

The debt commitments of institutions such as states, provinces, municipalities, and companies are known as bonds. Purchasing a bond means that you own a portion of an entity's liability and are eligible to collect regular interest payments and refund the bond's face value when it matures. Basically, by purchasing a bond, you are lending the government or a company money. They have to pay this money back to you with interest. If you want a more stable form of investment in comparison to stocks and shares for your family, bonds are your best bet. This is because they offer more stability. However, they typically offer lower returns than stocks in most cases. Bonds also face some investment risks which include repayment risk, credit risk, and interest rate risk.

Mutual Funds

Mutual funds are collective investments that allow shareholders to invest in bonds, stocks, chosen shares, and commodities. Exchange-traded funds (ETFs) and mutual funds are the two most popular forms of funds. In essence, a mutual fund involves a portfolio of stocks, shares, bonds, and debt which multiple investors can invest in. This is helpful due to the fact that multiple investors are pooling their money together into one portfolio. Therefore, if you don't have enough money to invest, the other parties make it possible for you to have a slice of the pie. The level of risk in a mutual fund is dependent on the investments in the fund.

Investment Trusts

Similarly, to mutual funds, investment trusts also involve pooling funds together. The most popular trusts are Real Estate Investment Trusts (REITs). These have to do with investing in domestic or industrial assets. They pay steady dividends from these assets' rental profits to their shareholders. REITs trade on stock markets and thereby give the benefit of immediate liquidity to their investors.

Alternative Investments

This type of investment consists of private equity investment and, of course, hedge funds. They are called hedge funds because they can hedge their portfolio stakes through various investments. The market can be unpredictable and hedge funds work to avoid this uncertainty and protect investments. It's basically an emergency fund but for massive corporations. Without going public, private equity allows businesses to raise capital. In the past, private equity and hedge funds were only open to wealthier individuals considered to be accredited investors who met the criteria for net worth and incomes. However, alternative investments have been launched in recent years that are open to institutional investors such as banks or credit unions.

Commodities

Commodities include metals, oil, grain, animal products, financial instruments, and currencies. They may either be exchanged through exchange-traded funds or through commodity futures contracts, which is an agreement to acquire or sell a certain amount of a commodity at a given price at a specific time in the future. Commodities can be used for hedge risk or speculative purposes. Similar to hedge funds, investing in commodities works to mitigate the uncertainty of the market. Therefore, if war, famine or drought strikes, the market price will be protected. However, these are high-risk investments and shouldn't be invested in lightly. For now, stick to stocks and bonds.

Comparing the Different Types of Investments

As you can see, investments come in many forms. However, some might be more beneficial for your family than others. Especially if you are just starting out, you don't want to throw all of your money into an investment that may fail. That is why it is important to understand what kind of investment option suits you and your family's needs.

- **Passive Investment vs. Active Investment**

An active investment allows you to control your investments. Usually, you would require a financial advisor to organize this, but essentially, active investments put you in control of buying and selling stocks and shares. On the flip side, passive investment, like a mutual fund, requires less input on your end as they will work to outgrow the market without your input. Although there are advantages and disadvantages to both methods, few portfolio managers exceed their targets regularly enough to warrant greater active management costs. If you are starting out, a passive investment may be the best option for you.

- **Growth vs. Value**

Growth investors tend to invest in high-growth businesses that have greater valuation ratios (showing the price you pay for financial metrics such as earning streams, cash flow, and revenues), such as a higher Price-to-Earnings ratio (PE). The PE ratio refers to how much the investor will get for their investment. For example, if you invest $1, then you may get $2 in return. You want to earn more than what you are investing; otherwise, you will end up losing money. Value companies have a much lower PE ratio and greater investment returns than growth companies. Depending on your needs, it may be wise to consult a financial advisor to determine whether you should invest in growth or value investments.

How to Invest

The topic of how to invest depends on whether you are a DIY (do-it-yourself) sort of investor or if you like your investments to be handled by a financial professional. Many investors who opt for self-management have accounts at discount brokerages due to their decreased commissions and the simplicity of carrying out trades. Investors who opt for expert money management tend to hire the services of funds managers who track their investments. These fund managers normally charge their customers a proportion of Assets Under Management or AUM as their charges. While expert money management is pricier than self-management of your money, investors hiring the services of an expert will also be paying for the convenience of assigning the research and decision-making process of the trading and investment to a professional. Choosing which option will depend on your comfort with investments and the control you want to have. It's in your best interest to keep informed of how your portfolio is doing. The latter may be a better option if you won't have the time to dedicate. However, if you want to save costs, the DIY route is the best way to go.

As you can see there are many ways you can actively and intentionally start to build wealth for your family. Beginning the process of investing can be intimidating at first, especially with the overly technical language and the fast pace of market trends. However, part of being financially successful is taking risks. Becoming comfortable with investments such as shares, mutual funds, stocks, bonds, commodities, small businesses, real estate, precious metals, or a mixture of all of the above can change the direction of your family's wealth building trajectory for the better.

Managing Investment Goals

Money provides a natural starting point for investment planning since you can't invest money you don't have. If you're a young person, your first task should be to make choices regarding retirement contributions, money market accounts, and savings. You may be middle-aged before realizing that life is moving very fast, and you need to start thinking of a retirement plan. Know that all investments begin with one dollar, whatever your age, income, or outlook. That said, people who have been investing for years do have the upper hand so start investing soon.

If you aim to send your children to university or want to retire on a Mediterranean yacht, investment is key to achieving your financial goals. The main thing to note is time—yes, you could lose capital in the short term, but you can gain wealth in the long run. But that is far away and it can be difficult to prioritize things that are so out of reach. However, it is still necessary to play the long game, so here are some of the benefits and reasons you should educate yourself about investments and investing your money.

- **Failing to understand investments increases the likelihood of failure.**

Investing your hard-earned money is a risk. You want to ensure that you reduce your risk of failure as much as possible. Take the time to learn even the basics of investing. You do not want to run the risk of losing your investments if you do not take your time to study the industry that you are thinking of investing in. If you feel lost, try consulting a financial advisor to make sure you are making the right decisions. Even so, it will be to your benefit to have a better and more informed discussion with your advisor when you take the time to do your investment research.

- **Investments can yield large returns.**

Investing produces far better rewards than simply keeping capital in a bank account. Yes, the stock market will experience highs and lows, but over time, your returns will grow and you will see the growth in your investments.

- **Asset diversification.**

The trick to investing is not to put all of your eggs in one basket. You shouldn't store all of your assets in cash or your house. Investing should make up one aspect of the financial picture—not everything. You are expected to have a decent amount of money (your emergency savings), real estate (your residence), tangible assets (your car and other items), and finally, your investments. Dispersing your assets can provide security for unexpected events in your life. If you keep all of your money in a savings account and that account gets drained then you will have nothing left. But if you have some investments, assets, property, your money will be safer for the future. This can keep you and your family financially secure for years to come.

- **The power of compounding.**

Compound interest is what increases your financial gains. Instead of using the interest your savings account or investments creates, you put that money back into the investment or savings account and gain even more interest on your money.

- **Because it works.**

People have been investing for hundreds of years, maybe not in the stock market as we know it today but in other ways. They have tried and tested aspects of investment that you might even think is nonsensical – but a least they tried and now you can learn from their experiences. Using this knowledge and information can guide you in your own financial investment journey. One rule that the most successful investors of all-time follow is that you can't foresee the future. There is no need to reinvent the wheel because many of the questions and challenges you are going to encounter have been solved by someone else. Your best bet is to study what has been done before and what works for you and incorporate it into your investment plan.

- **You will stop exchanging your time for money when you invest.**

Perhaps, this is the single most important advantage of investing. Because time is money, most regular employment will usually pay you in exchange for your time and expertise. But the perk of investing is that it can earn you money without taking much of your time or effort. So, your goal is to find a suitable investment that you can leverage and make the desired level of income without committing your whole day to it.

- **You beat inflation.**

Inflation is the increase in price over a certain period. If you look back over the past twenty years, you will notice that most commodities and services have increased in their price even though the value they provide may remain the same. Most estimates suggest that inflation increases at the rate of 3% every year, and it has shown to be consistently true. Investing is a better alternative to savings because it yields higher returns. This is because the interest you can earn from savings will be far lower than the rate of inflation (which will be reflected in your investments because they are in the real-world). When you save, it means that you are losing 3% of your purchasing power every year courtesy of inflation.

If you are feeling intimidated and confused in the world of investing, fear not. There are experts worldwide who have been trained to help you. Investing is a great way to build wealth for your family and gain financial freedom. However, it is not something you can do blindly. Figure out which kind of investments will work for you using your family and financial values and make sure you are making sound and practical financial decisions.

Chapter 8

How to Retire Early and Comfortably

"Don't simply retire from something; have something to retire to."

—Harry Emerson Fosdick

If you are like most people, you have probably thought about retiring early. You might not be cut-out for the rat race. Do you live for the weekends? How do you feel when Monday comes around? Retiring early is a possibility but you have to start planning early – this is key. Don't worry; you don't have to put 30% of your monthly income into a retirement fund. Putting a small amount in every month consistently overtime can set you up for the future and even allow you to retire early. Here are four steps to get you started on preparing for a successful retirement.

1. Evaluate your retirement expenses.

The first step is determining the amount of money you can pay per month for a retirement fund. If you have set out your budget and determined your monthly income and expenditures, be sure to take out 2-5% for your retirement fund every month. Optimally, you will enter retirement without any debt. That means no mortgage, no unpaid medical expenses, no credit card debt, and no student loans or other debt. Following the strategies provided in the book will help you live a debt-free and financially stable life and set you up for your retirement. Bear in mind that when you approach various retirement stages, your spending and priorities may change. This is why it is important to be aware of your goals and make sure to adapt them to your family's needs as you move through life.

2. Approximate the amount you will need for retirement.

Now that you have an idea of your budget, estimating how much you need to save is the next step. Using your monthly budget, work out your estimated annual spending and multiply it by the number of years you have until you retire. Remember to include an estimate of your emergency funds and debt. You have to know how much you need for retirement to determine the amount you should be saving. If you don't have a goal, you might have to work for ten more years before you can retire. As famous boxer and entrepreneur George Foreman once said, "the question isn't at what age I want to retire; it's at what income." Make sure you have an idea of where you are going.

3. Change your current spending habits.

It boils down to discipline. Many people who wish to retire early survive on 50% (or less) of their earnings. The rest is used to pay off debt and save. You have three choices in this case:

- Spend less
- Earn more
- Do both

Consult your budget to see where you can spend less and start applying to jobs that pay more. If that is not an option, take up a side hustle and start earning more money. The more you earn and the less you spend the faster you will be able to retire.

4. **Partner with a Financial Advisor.**

It's a smart idea to consult a financial planner because they will help you develop an investment plan to set you up for the future and perhaps even help you retire earlier. Your consultant can also help you monitor your retirement fund after you have retired to make sure you are actively earning money and not spending all of it. Income sources could include social assistance, required minimum distributions, dividend income, investing in real estate, and defined-benefit plans. Make sure to find a consultant you are comfortable with. After all, they might be managing your finances for years to come. When you are thinking about a financial planner's costs, note that you don't just pay for their time; you also pay for their experience. If you choose the best advisor, the cost may be higher but you won't be disappointed with their service.

The Benefits of Early Retirement

Planning for retirement includes paying a certain amount to the retirement account. We all have reasons for retiring early. You might want to spend more time with your family. You might want to travel and see the world. Figuring out why you may want to retire early will help you stay motivated and confident in your financial progress. Regardless of the reason, you need to prepare for it if you want to retire without experiencing any financial challenges when the time comes. 60% of people in Canada invest in retirement funds but not skillfully and 78% of Americans said that they are nervous about the amount of money they have saved for retirement. So, to avoid the stress and anxiety around retirement funds, here are a few reasons why retiring early is a good idea:

- **Early retirement means more freedom.**

Who doesn't like the idea of retiring early and spending the summer on a beach? This can become your reality if you make retirement plans. When other people are still busy working their lives away, you can be somewhere enjoying yourself with your family and loved ones. It is a healthy financial habit to start this process in your early twenties so that when you get to your fifties, you can retire comfortably.

- **You have options for investment.**

There are different options for you to increase the amount of money in your retirement fund. You can save part of it to live off for ten years and use the rest to invest and receive monthly dividends (which will basically act as an income in retirement). If you are strategic about your investments, you can get paid for being retired. That's the dream, isn't it?

- **You have fewer responsibilities.**

If you start saving for your retirement fund when you're younger, you will likely be able to save a reasonable amount before you get married and have children. At that stage you will likely have dependents who rely on you financially and saving will become more of a stretch. Suddenly, the utility bills become higher, and you'll have to shop for three or four more people. That is why it is important to start saving before you have other responsibilities. Think of it as a down payment on your retirement. The more you save when you are younger, the less you will have to contribute later in life.

- **You will retire with a solid foundation.**

The amount of money that you accrue in your account after retirement is directly proportional to the length of time that you have been saving. If you start earlier, say when you are in your twenties, thirties, or forties, you will have more funds in your retirement account than if you were to start a few years before retiring.

- **Your family will have something to fall back on.**

If you invested when you were younger, you would likely have enough funds to support your family indefinitely. Plus, if something happens to you, like injury or death, your partner and children can have extra financial reassurance with the fund you have set up together. If you have a family, it is important to plan for the future and make sure that you will all be comfortable and financially stable.

Tips on Saving Money for Retirement

Just establishing a retirement plan is not sufficient; you actually have to implement this strategy. Even with the most effective strategy, you might still struggle to stick to it and implement it into your daily life. Here are some effective tips that you can use to help you invest more effectively:

- **Monitor your investments.** Before you retire, be sure to invest in opportunities that have predictable results. Also, make sure that you invest in a few high-risk ventures because they will likely yield better results, but you also don't want to spend all of your money on something that might not work.

- **Formulate a budget.** Of course, you need a budget. By now, you should be tired of hearing it. But the point has to be reinforced. You need a budget to be aware of monthly expenses and make sure you stay on track.

- **Pay off loans.** Car loans, debt, mortgage, and other borrowed money that you may have. If you do this early, you won't have to pay the debt when you retire. It also frees up the money available to you in your retirement.

- **Make plans for unforeseen circumstances.** By keeping some funds aside for emergencies, you won't have to use your retirement fund.

- **Reduce your credit card usage.** This will help you monitor the money you have and make sure you don't pick up extra debt.

- **Keep the utility bills lower than they should be.** For instance, you can turn off the lights when you are not in the room or use water more sparingly. Again, common sense. But spending less will help you save more and set yourself up for retirement.

Chapter 9

How to Prioritize Your Final Wishes

"If a child, a spouse, a life partner, or a parent depends on you and your income, you need life insurance."

—Suze Orman

Many people tend to avoid the topic of life insurance, but this is an important issue because unexpected things can happen. If you lose your life as a primary financial contributor to your household without a plan for your loved ones, they could be left with overwhelming financial responsibilities. This is where life insurance can help. Life insurance policies are an agreement between a policyholder (you) and an insurer (the insurance company) in which the beneficiaries (your loved ones) of the policyholder receive payment when you die. The insurance company will pay a death benefit to the beneficiaries of this contract in exchange for a premium that the policymaker pays to the insurer. This means if you get a life insurance policy and lose your life due to unforeseen circumstances, your beneficiaries will get the financial payout.

The contract can become invalid after a certain period (like after retirement) unless you opt for a whole life insurance policy, in which case the policy will expire if you cancel it or upon death.

Who Should Have Life Insurance?

Life insurance provides a lump sum financial payment to surviving beneficiaries in the event of death. If you have any children, it is a good idea to look into life insurance. I know it can be uncomfortable for some to discuss but look at it as though it is a part of your financial plan. It is just another eventuality that you have to plan for. Wouldn't you rather know your family will have an additional source of income in the event that an unexpected loss occurs? Here are some recommendations for who should consider having life insurance:

- **Parents of young children.** If a parent dies, it usually results in a loss of income that now needs to be replaced. When a parent takes out a life insurance policy, their kids will have something to fall back on even if the parents are no longer there.

- **Parents with adult children who have special needs.** Children who need to be taken care of into adulthood will likely require funds to cover the costs of their medical and care expenses. A life insurance policy will make sure they are protected and secure even when the caregiver passes away.

- **Families that can't afford funeral and burial expenses.** A small life insurance policy can provide funds to honor the passing of a loved one. This also means that you won't have to dip into your savings to provide a funeral.

- **Married pensioners.** Rather than picking between pension payments that provide a benefit to a spouse and a pension payment that does not, a pensioner can decide to receive their complete pension and utilize some of the funds to purchase life insurance for their spouse. This is known as pension maximization.

- **Partners who co-own a property.** Your untimely death may mean that your partner will not have the funds to make the requisite payments for property taxes, upkeeps, and loan payments attached to a co-owned property alone. As such, life insurance can be a good solution.

The Modus Operandi of Life Insurance

Almost anyone can and should take out life insurance if they have dependents that would be affected by their passing. But how does life insurance actually work? Here are a few of the components to life insurance policies that you need to be aware of:

Death Benefit

The sum of money that the insurance provider gives to the recipients listed in the contract when the insured dies is known as a death benefit. The insured person could be a parent, and, for example, the beneficiaries could be their children. The insured will select the amount depending on the projected potential needs of the recipients the preferred death benefits. The insurance provider assesses if an insurable risk exists and whether the prospective insured individual is eligible for compensation on the grounds of the underwriting provisions of the company relating to age, fitness, and any risky activities in which the insured takes part.

Premiums

Premiums are the funds payable by the policyholder. When the policyholder passes away, the insurance company must pay the death benefit. Premiums are measured by how probable it is that the insurance company would have to pay the death benefit of the policy based on the life span of the insured.

Factors impacting average lifespan include workplace risks, medical records, sex, age, and high-risk activities of the insured. Half of the premium also contributes to the running costs of the insurance provider. Premiums have more regulations with larger death benefits. Participants who are at greater health risk will likely have to pay more as they are more likely to pass away. At the same time, policyholders who live healthy lives and rarely engage in risky activities such as smoking and drinking will be able to pay less and receive more benefits.

Cash Value

Cash value is the part of a whole life insurance policy that earns interest and may be available for withdrawal or borrow against in case of an emergency. It acts as a savings account that is usable by the policyholder during their lifespan. Such plans may have withdrawal limits based on how the funds should be used. The cash value is a living benefit that, until the insured dies, stays with the insurance provider. Any pending loans against the cash valuation would decrease the death benefit of the policy.

Types of Life Insurance

Life insurance policies come in many different shapes and sizes, and they are all tailored to meet your preferences and specific needs. So, the option you choose depends on why you need the policy in the first place.

- **Term life:** This type of insurance policy is valid for a certain number of years, after which it automatically terminates. The choice of the term when deploying the policy is yours to make. Popular terms last for ten, twenty, or even thirty years. The best term life insurance policies strike a balance between long-term financial capability and affordability.

- **Level term:** In this type of life insurance policy, the premiums remain unchanged every year.

- **Increasing term:** In increasing term life insurance policy, the premiums are less when you are younger and surge as you grow older. Another name for this type of insurance policy is known as a *yearly renewable term*.

- **Permanent:** This type of life insurance policy is effective for the insured's whole life unless they surrender the policy or stop paying the premiums. This policy tends to be more expensive than others.
- **Single-premium:** In the single-premium scenario, the policyholder pays the whole premium upfront rather than making annual, quarterly, or monthly payments.

- **Whole life:** This type of life insurance policy is a form of permanent life insurance that accrues cash value.

- **Universal life:** Universal life is a type of life insurance with cash value elements that receive interest. It also has premiums that are similar to term life insurance. Unlike whole and term life, the death benefit and premiums can be changed over time.

- **Guaranteed universal:** Guaranteed universal is a type of life insurance that does not create cash value and naturally has lower premiums when compared to the premiums of whole life insurance.

- **Variable universal:** With this type of life insurance policy, the insured is permitted to invest the policy's cash value.

- **Indexed universal:** Indexed universal is a type of life insurance policy that allows the insured to earn an equity-indexed or fixed return rate on the cash value.

- **Final or burial expense:** Final or burial expense is a type of life insurance policy that has a low death benefit. Regardless of the names, recipients can utilize the death benefit as they want.

- **Guaranteed issue:** Guaranteed issue is a typical life insurance policy that is accessible to individuals with medical problems that would typically make them uninsurable. This type of insurance policy will not make any death benefit payments during the first two years when the policy is active as a result of the increased risk of covering the individual. But then, the insurance provider will return the interest and policy premiums to the recipients if the policyholder dies during that time.

Additional Benefits of Life Insurance

Most individuals use life insurance to provide their family with money after they die so that they do not experience a financial burden. Nevertheless, other strategic options may be provided by the tax benefits of insurance policies, like tax-free death benefits, tax-free dividends, and tax-deferred cash value growth for wealthier people.

Funding retirement. Policies with an investment component or cash value can deliver a source of retirement earnings. This change will come with great premiums and a smaller death payout. It is only a decent choice for those who have maxed out most investment and savings accounts that are tax-advantaged. One other method that a life insurance policy can be used to fund retirement is the pension maximization approach mentioned earlier.

To stop taxation. A life insurance policy's death payment is typically tax-exempt. In a trust, some families often buy lifetime life insurance to cover the estate taxes that will be owed following their death. This method helps their dependents maintain the worth of the properties. This is a law-backed solution to reducing one's tax obligation, which cannot be mistaken with criminal tax evasion.

Cash Borrowing. The cash benefit that the policyholder may borrow against is accrued for most lifelong life insurance. Theoretically, you borrow money from the insurance firm and use it as security for your cash worth. Unlike other loans, the credit score of the policyholder is not a consideration. Repayment policies can be adjustable, and the interest on the debt falls back into the cash value account of the policyholder. Policy debt will, however, lower the death benefit of the policy.

Writing Your Last Will and Testament

A last will and testament is a legal document communicating the last wishes of an individual relating to their dependents, properties and assets. The last will and testament of a person specifies what to do with assets and whether the departed will give them to another party. It includes what will happen to the possessions of the deceased as well as other items for which they are responsible such as interest management, bank accounts, and custody of dependents.

A last will and testament will ensure your property is distributed to members of your family that you have appointed in the event of your death. This is very important and can help avoid financial problems for your family if you pass away. You should document your will while you are alive, and when you pass away, your wishes will be enforced. A will must identify a person who is still alive as the executor of your estate, and that person is in charge of managing your estate. Both you and your partner should have a last will and testament.

Key things to note

- If you die without writing a will your inheritance will be handled by the courts.
- Writing a last will and testament gives you more power over what becomes of your estate.

A last will and testament guides the court with regard to the disposal of all properties, including who is to obtain them and in what sum. For any specific cases, it provides guardian provisions for remaining accounts and dependents, which may feature the care of an elderly adult or a child with special needs. When a person becomes mentally or physically impaired, changes to the will, such as a medical order or a power of attorney, will direct the court on how to handle such cases.

The Implications of Not Writing a Will and Testament

If a person dies without a legitimate will, the state or province will appoint an administrator responsible for taking on the role of an executor. In sharing the property, the state or province determines how to divide it and who first collects payment, without taking into account the conditions and intricacies of a family. Any blood relation can, therefore, claim the property. Depending on the state or province's decision as to the beneficiary's best interests, the court may also adopt guardianship agreements. When a court finds that a will is wrongly written, it can declare it as void. Then the disposal of the property is liable to the intestate rule of the land.

Therefore, if you want your will to be executed after your death you have to make sure it is legitimate. This can be done through a lawyer. You will also need a witness to sign your last will and testament to make it legitimate. This avoids instances of fraud and malpractice and aims to protect the person and their wishes. In addition, setting up a legitimate will means that everyone gets what you want them to get. This avoids the possibility of your estranged brother coming to collect all of your property even though you want your children to own these assets. Just like you have been securing your future with life insurance policies, retirement plans and investments, make sure all of your accounts are settled and organized. Living a debt-free and financially secure life does not end with you if you have a family and dependents to consider. This is a very high-level overview of a process that can be complicated and intricate as families themselves. I therefore recommend that you and your partner consult with a lawyer before creating a last will and testament so that you carefully discuss and contemplate all possible considerations.

Conclusion

It might feel like you have a lot to think about, and you do, but if you take it one step at a time and follow the right paths, living a financially secure life will become a possibility for you. Some of the most important steps in this book are defining your family and financial goals and budgeting. Don't be worried if your budget doesn't work out the first few times. Constructing an accurate budget will take some trial and error but once you have a budget that you can follow, your road to a debt-free life will be much smoother. Financial planning is like creating a map of your finances. You have to know where you want to go, where you are, and how you are going to get there.

Remember that building wealth and acquiring financial freedom is not an easy task. It is something that takes a lot of time and commitment. Don't expect to see results immediately, especially if you have acquired a lot of debt over the years. Things like clearing a debt and saving cash for you and your family are a gradual process. It could take weeks, months, or even years before you have paid off all your debt. However, this does not mean it is impossible. Planning your finances and following the steps and advice provided in this book will put you on the fast-track to financial stability. Even though it may take a long time, it would probably take a lot longer if you didn't set up a financial plan and define your goals.

This journey may not always be linear but when times get tough, try to remember why you wanted to read this book. Ultimately, even with all of the information provided, living a financially comfortable and debt-free life is about the choices you make. You are probably here because of the poor financial choices you have made in the past. To change this, you have to be dedicated to your goals and the future of your family. You can decide to borrow money to buy a new car with high interest payments, or you can save up the money in cash and buy two cars in a couple years and no payments. Instead of conforming to instant gratification and the idea of *newness,* try approaching your financial situation in a calculated and intentional way.

You also don't know what might happen in the future. That is why emergency funds, savings accounts, rainy day funds, and sinking funds are so important to your financial situation. Life insurance policies and retirement plans will make sure you and your family are in a secure financial position even after something unexpected has happened to you. Don't underestimate the amount of time-saving it can take. Start as soon as possible and if you have to, start small.

While debt is a part of many people's lives, try to avoid it at all costs. Credit cards will give you a false sense of security; however, if used sparingly, they can be a very useful financial tool. And although saving is a priority, paying off your debt should be your main focus; otherwise, all the money you saved will have to go towards paying those debts as well as interest. Remember to adapt your goals as you move through this financial journey. You want to make sure you don't stagnate. If you get a big promotion at work and your income suddenly increases, sticking to your old goals and budgets won't give you the full benefit of the extra money you are earning.

If you are looking to build wealth, investing is the way to go. You can either do it yourself or find a financial advisor that has your best interest in mind. There are many different ways to invest, so just like with saving, start slow and if you have to, start small. Investing can be a risky venture but if done right, the rewards can be life-changing. This is a great way to make your money grow for you and help you pay off debts. You might also be so successful that you find you can live off the interest of your investments and save your income. The possibilities are endless; you just have to find one that works for you.

Everything you need to turn your family's financial outlook around has been carefully detailed in this book. And if you follow all of the tips and suggestions as they apply to your situation, your family can get the financial freedom they deserve. By committing to a financial plan based on your family's financial values you will be solidifying your finances and propelling your family's future wealth and security for generations to come. Remember that you can do this; just stay committed and stay the course. Before you know it, one day you'll revisit that cafe where you once struggled to buy a couple of drinks. Only this time you confidently walk in knowing that you have more than enough to pay for a few iced beverages because you budgeted spending money in your sinking fund this month. And what's even more impressive is that your little ones offer to pay for their drinks from the money they took out of their piggy bank this morning. Well done!

References

Administration for Children and Families. (2019). How does child support work? https://www.acf.hhs.gov/css/parents/how-does-child-support-work.

Bank, E. (2019). The advantages of the presence of a sinking fund. Finance. https://finance.zacks.com/advantages-presence-sinking-fund-7682.html.

Barrett, J. (2020). 6 side hustles you can do from home to earn extra money. Forbes. https://www.forbes.com/sites/jenniferbarrett/2020/11/16/6-side-hustles-you-can-do-from--home-to-earn-extra-money/?sh=7d5ab9db470c.

Cain, S., L. (2020). The 6 best budgeting software of 2020. https://www.investopedia.com/personal-finance/best-budgeting-software/.

Caldwell, M. (2019). 8 reasons you need an emergency fund now. The Balance. https://www.thebalance.com/reasons-you-need-an-emergency-fund-2385536.

Caldwell, M. (2020). Do these 20 things right now to improve your finances. The Balance. https://www.thebalance.com/get-control-of-finances-2386026.

Chapkanovska, E. (2020). 17+ consumer spending statistics to know in 2020.

https://spendmenot.com/blog/consumer-spending-statistics/.

Chrissy. (2020). Top 10 tips to get your finances organised. Organise My House. https://organisemyhouse.com/top-10-tips-to-get-your-finances-organised/.

Colley, S. (2016). Non-negotiable budget categories. Financial Help Desk. https://financialhelpdesk.com/2016/10/07/non-negotiable-budget-categories-budgeting/.

Fay, B. (2020). Consumer debt statistics & demographics in America. Debt. https://www.debt.org/faqs/americans-in-debt/demographics/.

Financial Post. (2014). Couples More Willing to Forgive Spouse for Cheating than Money Problems, BMO Survey Finds. https://financialpost.com/personal-finance/couples-more-willing-to-forgive-spouse-for-cheating-than-money-problems-bmo-survey-finds.

Fuscaldo, D. (2019). Most Americans struggling financially despite the strong economy. Forbes. https://www.forbes.com/sites/donnafuscaldo/2019/11/15/most-americans-struggling-financially-despite-the-strong-economy/.

Gallo, L. (2015). Speaking of Psychology: The stress of money. American Psychological Association. https://www.apa.org/research/action/speaking-of-psychology/financial-stress.

Gellerman, E. (2019). What is a sinking fund and why do you need it? Chime. https://www.chime.com/blog/what-is-a-sinking-fund-and-why-do-you-need-it/.

Graves, S. (2020). Family vacation benefits. Money Crashers. https://www.moneycrashers.com/family-vacations-benefits/.

Hamm, T. (2017). 20 reasons why you need an emergency fund. The Simple Dollar. https://www.thesimpledollar.com/save-money/20-reasons-why-you-need-an-emergency-fund/.

Hervey, J., C. (2018). Why your budget is a mirror of your values. Forbes. https://www.forbes.com/sites/janeclairehervey/2018/11/29/why-your-budget-is-a-mirror-of-your-values/?sh=7e5878114ee0.

Holton, L. J. (2020). Financial literacy and career resources. iGrad. https://www.igrad.com/articles/the-benefits-of-using-technology-to-help-manage-your-money.

LaPonsie, M. (2020). How to create and maintain a family budget. US News. https://money.usnews.com/money/personal-finance/saving-and-budgeting/articles/how-to-make-a-family-budget.

Lincoln, T. (2020). 15 powerful reasons why you should invest in the stock market. Medium. https://medium.com/the-post-grad-survival-guide/15-powerful-reasons-why-you-should-invest-in-the-stock-market-b1c155370313.

Maddox, C. (2020). A guide on how to figure out budget percentages. Chime. https://www.chime.com/blog/recommended-budget-category-percentages/.

Milton, S. (2020). Conscious vs. unconscious spending. Retire Happy. https://retirehappy.ca/conscious-vs-unconscious-spending/.

Money and Mental Health. (N.d.). Money and mental health facts and statistics - A Money and Mental Health Policy. https://www.moneyandmentalhealth.org/money-and-mental-health-facts/.

Money Habitudes. (2019). Financial statistics. https://www.moneyhabitudes.com/financial-statistics/.

PR Newswire. (2019). Fewer Americans are budgeting in 2019–Although they think everyone else should. https://www.prnewswire.com/news-releases/fewer-americans-are-budgeting-in-2019----although-they-think-everyone-else-should-300824384.html.

Schroeder-Gardner, M. (2018). 10 statistics about the money habits of the average American. Making Sense of Cents. https://www.makingsenseofcents.com/2018/04/money-habits.html.

Sloan, K. (2018). 4 ways to use technology to improve your budget. Due. https://due.com/blog/technology-improve-your-budget/.

Smith, L. (2020). What is a will and why do I need one now? Investopedia. https://www.investopedia.com/articles/pf/08/what-is-a-will.asp.

Town, P. (2020). 6 types of investments (to make the most money): Rule #1 investing. Rule One Investing. https://www.ruleoneinvesting.com/blog/how-to-invest/types-of-investments/.

Tyll, K. (2018). How to write a last will and testament. Meet Fabric. https://meetfabric.com/blog/how-to-write-a-last-will-and-testament.

Walrack, J. (2020). How to save for your child's college education. The Simple Dollar. https://www.thesimpledollar.com/financial-wellness/how-to-save-for-your-childs-college-education/.

Whiteside, E. (2020). What is the 50/20/30 budget rule? Investopedia. https://www.investopedia.com/ask/answers/022916/what-502030-budget-rule.asp.

Williams, G. (2018). 10 steps to writing a will. U.S. News & World Report. https://money.usnews.com/money/personal-finance/family-finance/articles/steps-to-writing-a-will.

Wilson, T. (2020). Reasons for making a will. Which. https://www.which.co.uk/money/wills-and-probate/passing-on-your-money/reasons-for-making-a-will-a4mzh4b503jc.

Printed in Great Britain
by Amazon